"After utilizing toolkits from The Art of Service, I was able to identify threats within my organization to which I was completely unaware. Using my team's knowledge as a competitive advantage, we now have superior systems that save time and energy."

"As a new Chief Technology Officer, I was feeling unprepared and inadequate to be successful in my role. I ordered an IT toolkit Sunday night and was prepared Monday morning to shed light on areas of improvement within my organization. I no longer felt overwhelmed and intimidated, I was excited to share what I had learned."

"I used the questionnaires to interview members of my team. I never knew how many insights we could produce collectively with our internal knowledge."

"I usually work until at least 8pm on weeknights. The Art of Service questionnaire saved me so much time and worry that Thursday night I attended my son's soccer game without sacrificing my professional obligations."

"After purchasing The Art of Service toolkit, I was able to identify areas where my company was not in compliance that could have put my job at risk. I looked like a hero when I proactively educated my team on the risks and presented a solid solution."

"I spent months shopping for an external consultant before realizing that The Art of Service would allow my team to consult themselves! Not only did we save time not catching a consultant up to speed, we were able to keep our company information and industry secrets confidential."

"Everyday there are new regulations and processes in my industry. The Art of Service toolkit has kept me ahead by using AI technology to constantly update the toolkits and address emerging needs."

"I customized The Art of Service toolkit to focus specifically on the concerns of my role and industry. I didn't have to waste time with a generic self-help book that wasn't tailored to my exact situation."

"Many of our competitors have asked us about our secret sauce. When I tell them it's the knowledge we have in-house, they never believe me. Little do they know The Art of Service toolkits are working behind the scenes."

"One of my friends hired a consultant who used the knowledge gained working with his company to advise their competitor. Talk about a competitive disadvantage! The Art of Service allowed us to keep our knowledge from walking out the door along with a huge portion of our budget in consulting fees."

"Honestly, I didn't know what I didn't know. Before purchasing The Art of Service, I didn't realize how many areas of my business needed to be refreshed and improved. I am so relieved The Art of Service was there to highlight our blind spots."

"Before The Art of Service, I waited eagerly for consulting company reports to come out each month. These reports kept us up to speed but provided little value because they put our competitors on the same playing field. With The Art of Service, we have uncovered unique insights to drive our business forward."

"Instead of investing extensive resources into an external consultant, we can spend more of our budget towards pursuing our company goals and objectives…while also spending a little more on corporate holiday parties."

"The risk of our competitors getting ahead has been mitigated because The Art of Service has provided us with a 360-degree view of threats within our organization before they even arise."

Chief Revenue Officer
Complete Self-Assessment Guide

Table of Contents

About The Art of Service

The Art of Service, Business Process Architects since 2000, is dedicated to helping stakeholders achieve excellence.

Defining, designing, creating, and implementing a process to solve a stakeholders challenge or meet an objective is the most valuable role… In EVERY group, company, organization and department.

Unless you're talking a one-time, single-use project, there should be a process. Whether that process is managed and implemented by humans, AI, or a combination of the two, it needs to be designed by someone with a complex enough perspective to ask the right questions.

Someone capable of asking the right questions and step back and say, 'What are we really trying to accomplish here? And is there a different way to look at it?'

With The Art of Service's Self-Assessments, we empower people who can do just that — whether their title is marketer, entrepreneur, manager, salesperson, consultant, Business Process Manager, executive assistant, IT Manager, CIO etc... —they are the people who rule the future. They are people who watch the process as it happens, and ask the right questions to make the process work better.

Contact us when you need any support with this Self-Assessment and any help with templates, blue-prints and examples of standard documents you might need:

https://theartofservice.com
support@theartofservice.com

Included Resources - how to access

Included with your purchase of the book is the Chief Revenue

Officer Self-Assessment Spreadsheet Dashboard which contains all questions and Self-Assessment areas and auto-generates insights, graphs, and project RACI planning - all with examples to get you started right away.

How? Simply send an email to
access@theartofservice.com
with this books' title in the subject to get the Chief Revenue Officer Self Assessment Tool right away.

The auto reply will guide you further, you will then receive the following contents with New and Updated specific criteria:

• The latest quick edition of the book in PDF

• The latest complete edition of the book in PDF, which criteria correspond to the criteria in...

• The Self-Assessment Excel Dashboard, and...

• Example pre-filled Self-Assessment Excel Dashboard to get familiar with results generation

• In-depth specific Checklists covering the topic

• Project management checklists and templates to assist with implementation

Purpose of this Self-Assessment

This Self-Assessment has been developed to improve understanding of the requirements and elements of Chief Revenue Officer, based on best practices and standards in business process architecture, design and quality management.

It is designed to allow for a rapid Self-Assessment to determine how closely existing management practices and procedures correspond to the elements of the Self-Assessment.

The criteria of requirements and elements of Chief Revenue Officer have been rephrased in the format of a Self-Assessment questionnaire, with a seven-criterion scoring system, as explained in this document.

In this format, even with limited background knowledge of Chief Revenue Officer, a manager can quickly review existing operations to determine how they measure up to the standards. This in turn can serve as the starting point of a 'gap analysis' to identify management tools or system elements that might usefully be implemented in the organization to help improve overall performance.

How to use the Self-Assessment

On the following pages are a series of questions to identify to what extent your Chief Revenue Officer initiative is complete in comparison to the requirements set in standards.

To facilitate answering the questions, there is a space in front of each question to enter a score on a scale of '1' to '5'.

1 Strongly Disagree

2 Disagree

3 Neutral

4 Agree

5 Strongly Agree

Read the question and rate it with the following in front of mind:

'In my belief, the answer to this question is clearly defined'.

There are two ways in which you can choose to interpret this statement;
1. how aware are you that the answer to the question is clearly defined
2. for more in-depth analysis you can choose to gather evidence and confirm the answer to the question. This obviously will take more time, most Self-Assessment users opt for the first way to interpret the question and dig deeper later on based on the outcome of the overall Self-Assessment.

A score of '1' would mean that the answer is not clear at all, where a '5' would mean the answer is crystal clear and defined. Leave emtpy when the question is not applicable or you don't want to answer it, you can skip it without affecting your score. Write your score in the space provided.

After you have responded to all the appropriate statements in each section, compute your average score for that section, using the formula provided, and round to the nearest tenth. Then transfer to the corresponding spoke in the Chief Revenue Officer Scorecard on the second next page of the Self-Assessment.

Your completed Chief Revenue Officer Scorecard will give you a clear presentation of which Chief Revenue Officer areas need attention.

Chief Revenue Officer Scorecard Example

Example of how the finalized Scorecard can look like:

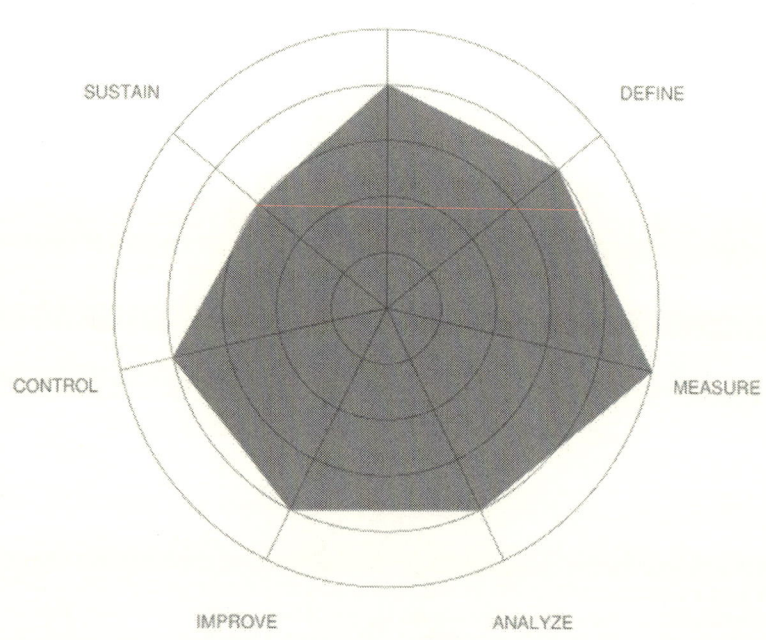

Chief Revenue Officer Scorecard

Your Scores:

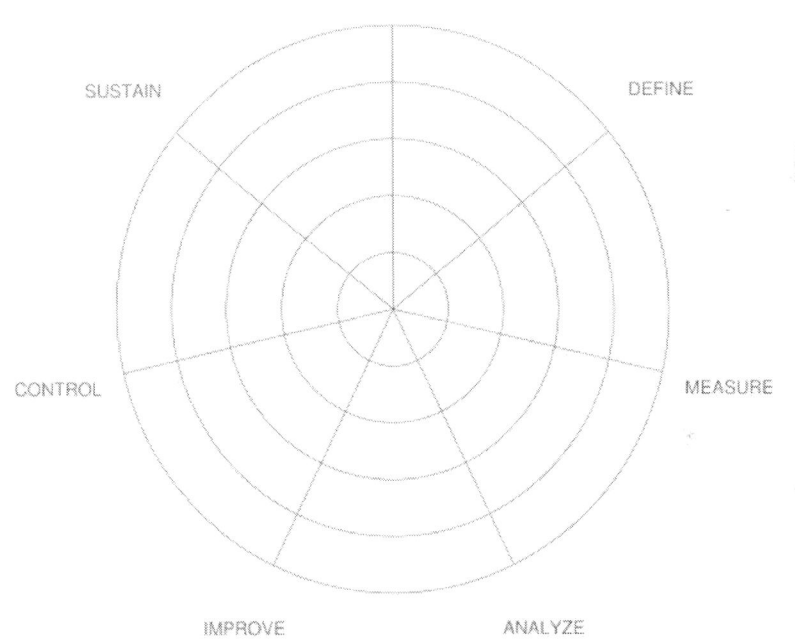

BEGINNING OF THE SELF-ASSESSMENT:

CRITERION #1: RECOGNIZE

INTENT: Be aware of the need for change. Recognize that there is an unfavorable variation, problem or symptom.

In my belief, the answer to this question is clearly defined:

5 Strongly Agree

4 Agree

3 Neutral

2 Disagree

1 Strongly Disagree

1. Does your organization know a problem exists?
<--- Score

2. Do you need to share personal goals?
<--- Score

3. Do your products and services serve evolving consumer needs?
<--- Score

4. Will Chief Revenue Officer deliverables need to be tested and, if so, by whom?
<--- Score

5. What creative shifts do you need to take?
<--- Score

6. Have feasibility or management problems emerged?
<--- Score

7. Who do you really need on the leadership team to implement the strategy?
<--- Score

8. What vendors make products that address the Chief Revenue Officer needs?
<--- Score

9. Does your organizations value depend on a brand truly recognized and valued by the customers?
<--- Score

10. How will customer needs evolve in the future?
<--- Score

11. Are employees recognized for desired behaviors?
<--- Score

12. Are controls defined to recognize and contain problems?
<--- Score

13. Are there any specific expectations or concerns

about the Chief Revenue Officer team, Chief Revenue Officer itself?

<--- Score

14. How much are sponsors, customers, partners, stakeholders involved in Chief Revenue Officer? In other words, what are the risks, if Chief Revenue Officer does not deliver successfully?

<--- Score

15. What kinds of professional tools, employee engagement strategies, and resources do department need to be on top of employee achievement?

<--- Score

16. As a sponsor, customer or management, how important is it to meet goals, objectives?

<--- Score

17. What are your needs in relation to Chief Revenue Officer skills, labor, equipment, and markets?

<--- Score

18. What are the steps a large, multinational organization should take to identify the most relevant sustainability issues important to its business success?

<--- Score

19. What is the recognized need?

<--- Score

20. Who else hopes to benefit from it?

<--- Score

21. What would happen if Chief Revenue Officer weren't done?
<--- Score

22. Why does the customer need the product?
<--- Score

23. What department have identified that employees should know and be able to do?
<--- Score

24. What are the Chief Revenue Officer resources needed?
<--- Score

25. Where does management need to allocate more resources?
<--- Score

26. How much time is spent in the finance function doing what no longer needs to be done?
<--- Score

27. What triggers corporate sustainability?
<--- Score

28. Are there any other relevant matters the committee needs to address?
<--- Score

29. Do you need regular reporting for compliance?
<--- Score

30. How has your team changed how you work with your departments to meet your needs?
<--- Score

31. What problems are you facing and how do you consider Chief Revenue Officer will circumvent those obstacles?
<--- Score

32. What situation(s) led to this Chief Revenue Officer Self Assessment?
<--- Score

33. What are the stakeholder objectives to be achieved with Chief Revenue Officer?
<--- Score

34. Are there any culture-related sensitivities or issues that may influence the outcome of procurement?
<--- Score

35. What are the expected benefits of Chief Revenue Officer to the stakeholder?
<--- Score

36. How are you going to measure success?
<--- Score

37. What Chief Revenue Officer capabilities do you need?
<--- Score

38. How do marketer capabilities and relationships need to change as disruptive technologies transform the marketing value chain?
<--- Score

39. Who needs budgets?

<--- Score

40. Does everyone in real estate sales need a coach?
<--- Score

41. How does the technology solve problems in a unique way?
<--- Score

42. What is the customer challenge or pain point that needs solving?
<--- Score

43. What insights do you have and need across the buying and selling journey?
<--- Score

44. What does Chief Revenue Officer success mean to the stakeholders?
<--- Score

45. What is the extent or complexity of the Chief Revenue Officer problem?
<--- Score

46. What problem does the technology address?
<--- Score

47. How are the Chief Revenue Officer's objectives aligned to the group's overall stakeholder strategy?
<--- Score

48. What is the biggest problem you see for the future?
<--- Score

49. What needs to stay?
<--- Score

Add up total points for this section:
_____ = Total points for this section

Divided by: _____ (number of
statements answered) = _____
Average score for this section

Transfer your score to the Chief Revenue
Officer Index at the beginning of the
Self-Assessment.

CRITERION #2: DEFINE:

INTENT: Formulate the stakeholder problem. Define the problem, needs and objectives.

In my belief, the answer to this question is clearly defined:

5 Strongly Agree

4 Agree

3 Neutral

2 Disagree

1 Strongly Disagree

1. What are the requirements around maintaining confidentiality of customers?
<--- Score

2. What are the boundaries of the scope? What is in bounds and what is not? What is the start point? What is the stop point?
<--- Score

3. Is the Chief Revenue Officer scope manageable?
<--- Score

4. Are stakeholder processes mapped?
<--- Score

5. Is there a completed, verified, and validated high-level 'as is' (not 'should be' or 'could be') stakeholder process map?
<--- Score

6. How do you keep key subject matter experts in the loop?
<--- Score

7. Has the direction changed at all during the course of Chief Revenue Officer? If so, when did it change and why?
<--- Score

8. What technical knowledge is required to run or manage the business?
<--- Score

9. Is the work to date meeting requirements?
<--- Score

10. Have all of the relationships been defined properly?
<--- Score

11. What is out of scope?
<--- Score

12. What key stakeholder process output measure(s) does Chief Revenue Officer leverage and how?

<--- Score

13. Are different versions of process maps needed to account for the different types of inputs?
<--- Score

14. What is the requirement around maintaining social equity employees for the long term?
<--- Score

15. Are audit criteria, scope, frequency and methods defined?
<--- Score

16. What are the core elements of the Chief Revenue Officer business case?
<--- Score

17. Has the Chief Revenue Officer work been fairly and/or equitably divided and delegated among team members who are qualified and capable to perform the work? Has everyone contributed?
<--- Score

18. Is there regularly 100% attendance at the team meetings? If not, have appointed substitutes attended to preserve cross-functionality and full representation?
<--- Score

19. What are the security requirements of your enterprise, customer or internal stakeholders?
<--- Score

20. Is the team sponsored by a champion or stakeholder leader?

<--- Score

21. Are improvement team members fully trained on Chief Revenue Officer?
<--- Score

22. Has/have the customer(s) been identified?
<--- Score

23. Do the hours of operation define when the dispensary is open to the public or the total hours employees are in the facility?
<--- Score

24. Who are the Chief Revenue Officer improvement team members, including Management Leads and Coaches?
<--- Score

25. Will you ensure business continuity in case of any interruption?
<--- Score

26. How did the Chief Revenue Officer manager receive input to the development of a Chief Revenue Officer improvement plan and the estimated completion dates/times of each activity?
<--- Score

27. Is the team adequately staffed with the desired cross-functionality? If not, what additional resources are available to the team?
<--- Score

28. How would your organization define sustainability that is relevant to its business?

<--- Score

29. How has your case mix/specialty mix changed over the years?
<--- Score

30. What are the requirements for claiming tax deductions for payments to family members for services?
<--- Score

31. When are meeting minutes sent out? Who is on the distribution list?
<--- Score

32. Do you have administration or management requirements for resources in different networks?
<--- Score

33. Why is it that few suppliers in business markets are able to define and measure value?
<--- Score

34. How will the Chief Revenue Officer team and the group measure complete success of Chief Revenue Officer?
<--- Score

35. How will variation in the actual durations of each activity be dealt with to ensure that the expected Chief Revenue Officer results are met?
<--- Score

36. What specifically is the problem? Where does it occur? When does it occur? What is its extent?
<--- Score

37. How is the team tracking and documenting its work?
<--- Score

38. Is Chief Revenue Officer linked to key stakeholder goals and objectives?
<--- Score

39. When is the estimated completion date?
<--- Score

40. Have the customer needs been translated into specific, measurable requirements? How?
<--- Score

41. What are the dynamics of the communication plan?
<--- Score

42. Is data collected and displayed to better understand customer(s) critical needs and requirements.
<--- Score

43. How was the 'as is' process map developed, reviewed, verified and validated?
<--- Score

44. How much of the owners time is required to run the business?
<--- Score

45. If substitutes have been appointed, have they been briefed on the Chief Revenue Officer goals and received regular communications as to the progress

to date?

<--- Score

46. What is required to conduct the business of the Annual Meeting?

<--- Score

47. How often are the team meetings?

<--- Score

48. Are there any licensing requirements in order to run the business?

<--- Score

49. Is diversity defined by nationality?

<--- Score

50. Is full participation by members in regularly held team meetings guaranteed?

<--- Score

51. Has a high-level 'as is' process map been completed, verified and validated?

<--- Score

52. What is the internal catalyst/business case that actually forces the change?

<--- Score

53. What are the Roles and Responsibilities for each team member and its leadership? Where is this documented?

<--- Score

54. What customer feedback methods were used to solicit their input?

<--- Score

55. Are there any constraints known that bear on the ability to perform Chief Revenue Officer work? How is the team addressing them?
<--- Score

56. When is/was the Chief Revenue Officer start date?
<--- Score

57. What are the rough order estimates on cost savings/opportunities that Chief Revenue Officer brings?
<--- Score

58. Do the problem and goal statements meet the SMART criteria (specific, measurable, attainable, relevant, and time-bound)?
<--- Score

59. Will team members perform Chief Revenue Officer work when assigned and in a timely fashion?
<--- Score

60. Is there a Chief Revenue Officer management charter, including stakeholder case, problem and goal statements, scope, milestones, roles and responsibilities, communication plan?
<--- Score

61. How do you communicate technical information when required?
<--- Score

62. What constraints exist that might impact the team?

<--- Score

63. Is a fully trained team formed, supported, and committed to work on the Chief Revenue Officer improvements?
<--- Score

64. What Chief Revenue Officer services do you require?
<--- Score

65. What would be the goal or target for a Chief Revenue Officer's improvement team?
<--- Score

66. Has the improvement team collected the 'voice of the customer' (obtained feedback – qualitative and quantitative)?
<--- Score

67. Are customers identified and high impact areas defined?
<--- Score

68. Has everyone on the team, including the team leaders, been properly trained?
<--- Score

69. What are the compelling stakeholder reasons for embarking on Chief Revenue Officer?
<--- Score

70. Are the goals of the project defined clearly?
<--- Score

71. What knowledge or experience is required?

<--- Score

72. How does the Chief Revenue Officer manager ensure against scope creep?
<--- Score

73. Is Chief Revenue Officer currently on schedule according to the plan?
<--- Score

74. Has a project plan, Gantt chart, or similar been developed/completed?
<--- Score

75. Are there different segments of customers?
<--- Score

76. How and when will the baselines be defined?
<--- Score

77. What are the requirements for an effective compliance program?
<--- Score

78. Are team charters developed?
<--- Score

79. Is the team formed and are team leaders (Coaches and Management Leads) assigned?
<--- Score

80. Are customer(s) identified and segmented according to their different needs and requirements?
<--- Score

81. What perspectives are required in your new

role?
<--- Score

82. Has anyone else (internal or external to the group) attempted to solve this problem or a similar one before? If so, what knowledge can be leveraged from these previous efforts?
<--- Score

83. Will team members regularly document their Chief Revenue Officer work?
<--- Score

84. Is the team equipped with available and reliable resources?
<--- Score

85. Has a team charter been developed and communicated?
<--- Score

86. Is there a critical path to deliver Chief Revenue Officer results?
<--- Score

87. What are the legally required elements of a compliance program?
<--- Score

88. Is the improvement team aware of the different versions of a process: what they think it is vs. what it actually is vs. what it should be vs. what it could be?
<--- Score

89. What critical content must be communicated – who, what, when, where, and how?

<--- Score

90. Is there a completed SIPOC representation, describing the Suppliers, Inputs, Process, Outputs, and Customers?
<--- Score

91. Does the team have regular meetings?
<--- Score

92. Is the current 'as is' process being followed? If not, what are the discrepancies?
<--- Score

Add up total points for this section:
_____ = Total points for this section

Divided by: _____ (number of statements answered) = _____
Average score for this section

Transfer your score to the Chief Revenue Officer Index at the beginning of the Self-Assessment.

CRITERION #3: MEASURE:

INTENT: Gather the correct data. Measure the current performance and evolution of the situation.

In my belief, the answer to this question is clearly defined:

5 Strongly Agree

4 Agree

3 Neutral

2 Disagree

1 Strongly Disagree

1. What particular quality tools did the team find helpful in establishing measurements?
<--- Score

2. What is the cause of any Chief Revenue Officer gaps?
<--- Score

3. Has a cost benefit analysis been performed?

<--- Score

4. Which customer touchpoints should budget and effort be focused on?
<--- Score

5. How does procurement adapt, when an advertisers focus on efficient reach is increasingly at odds with the way consumers want brands to behave?
<--- Score

6. What data was collected (past, present, future/ ongoing)?
<--- Score

7. What are the agreed upon definitions of the high impact areas, defect(s), unit(s), and opportunities that will figure into the process capability metrics?
<--- Score

8. Are business leaders focusing on short-term targets over long-term profitability?
<--- Score

9. What would trigger your organization to focus more on long-term strategy?
<--- Score

10. Have you found any 'ground fruit' or 'low-hanging fruit' for immediate remedies to the gap in performance?
<--- Score

11. How do you quantify and qualify impacts?
<--- Score

12. Does management have the right priorities among projects?
<--- Score

13. Are high impact defects defined and identified in the stakeholder process?
<--- Score

14. How do you go about setting priorities for your time?
<--- Score

15. How does email design impact content across the customer journey?
<--- Score

16. What are the top issues CFOs are focusing on to minimize risk?
<--- Score

17. Is a solid data collection plan established that includes measurement systems analysis?
<--- Score

18. What users will be impacted?
<--- Score

19. What is happening, what is going to happen and how will it impact your business?
<--- Score

20. How can legacy data and hardware be integrated onto modern platforms for analytics?
<--- Score

21. How large is the gap between current performance and the customer-specified (goal) performance?
<--- Score

22. Is there a Performance Baseline?
<--- Score

23. How do you verify the Chief Revenue Officer requirements quality?
<--- Score

24. How do you focus them on getting better at taking the right actions with the right people that lead to results?
<--- Score

25. What are the costs?
<--- Score

26. What do organization leaders need to know about data analytics and data management to improve employee outcomes and meet organizational goals?
<--- Score

27. Why is it so important to focus on one skill at a time?
<--- Score

28. How is the industry benefiting from data analytics?
<--- Score

29. How can strategy leaders make a greater impact?

<--- Score

30. How do you apply real-time analytics on business processes to support digital transformation?
<--- Score

31. How do you aggregate measures across priorities?
<--- Score

32. Why is it important to focus on one skill at a time?
<--- Score

33. Is data collected on key measures that were identified?
<--- Score

34. Are key measures identified and agreed upon?
<--- Score

35. What are the top trends, use cases and business benefits for customer analytics?
<--- Score

36. Can a new owner replicate the cost structure?
<--- Score

37. How do you select the right analytics and BI solutions for business users?
<--- Score

38. How are costs allocated?
<--- Score

39. What is the right balance of time and resources

between investigation, analysis, and discussion and dissemination?
<--- Score

40. What duties do you reprioritize or delegate in order to devote time to fostering new relationships?
<--- Score

41. What are the key environmental impacts or issues of the industry?
<--- Score

42. What factors had the greatest impact on the level of success for projects?
<--- Score

43. How is marketing measured primarily at your organization?
<--- Score

44. How do you focus on what is right -not who is right?
<--- Score

45. How will you measure your Chief Revenue Officer effectiveness?
<--- Score

46. How does your organization recognize the legal issues and manage the risks in a cost effective way?
<--- Score

47. What do you measure and why?
<--- Score

48. What key measures identified indicate the performance of the stakeholder process?
<--- Score

49. How long to keep data and how to manage retention costs?
<--- Score

50. What are hidden Chief Revenue Officer quality costs?
<--- Score

51. What factors prevent your organization from using marketing analytics more often in decision making?
<--- Score

52. Are process variation components displayed/ communicated using suitable charts, graphs, plots?
<--- Score

53. What needs to transform if you shift your focus from marketing effectiveness to connected customer experiences?
<--- Score

54. Was a data collection plan established?
<--- Score

55. What causes mismanagement?
<--- Score

56. What disadvantage does this cause for the user?
<--- Score

57. Have all non-recommended alternatives been analyzed in sufficient detail?
<--- Score

58. How do you stay flexible and focused to recognize larger Chief Revenue Officer results?
<--- Score

59. What are the strengths and weaknesses, priorities and risk?
<--- Score

60. What are the key input variables? What are the key process variables? What are the key output variables?
<--- Score

61. What metrics do you use to measure Sales and Marketing alignment?
<--- Score

62. Which operating model is more impactful?
<--- Score

63. What value can analytics add to operations if there is no solution for interoperability?
<--- Score

64. What impact is availability of key skills having on your organizations growth prospects?
<--- Score

65. What is the Chief Revenue Officer business impact?
<--- Score

66. How is the focus on customer retention

communicated internally?
<--- Score

67. Does a Chief Revenue Officer quantification method exist?
<--- Score

68. Is Process Variation Displayed/Communicated?
<--- Score

69. What would be the impact of a data breach in your organization?
<--- Score

70. How do you impact the business and drive performance with analytics?
<--- Score

71. How do you prioritize your time?
<--- Score

72. Which market segments do you focus on?
<--- Score

73. How will measures be used to manage and adapt?
<--- Score

74. What have been the biggest impacts to your business?
<--- Score

75. How do you quantify the results of your activities as a manager?
<--- Score

76. Is data collection planned and executed?

<--- Score

77. What happens if cost savings do not materialize?
<--- Score

78. Who participated in the data collection for measurements?
<--- Score

79. How do you verify and develop ideas and innovations?
<--- Score

80. Did you tackle the cause or the symptom?
<--- Score

81. How frequently do you track Chief Revenue Officer measures?
<--- Score

82. How does cost-to-serve analysis help?
<--- Score

83. Is key measure data collection planned and executed, process variation displayed and communicated and performance baselined?
<--- Score

84. Did you include specific results and quantifiable accomplishments in your experience section?
<--- Score

85. How much would the chosen technology cost?
<--- Score

86. What has the team done to assure the stability and accuracy of the measurement process?
<--- Score

87. Do analysts and auditors use information in accruals?
<--- Score

88. Is long term and short term variability accounted for?
<--- Score

89. What causes investor action?
<--- Score

90. How do you verify if Chief Revenue Officer is built right?
<--- Score

91. What charts has the team used to display the components of variation in the process?
<--- Score

92. Do staff have the necessary skills to collect, analyze, and report data?
<--- Score

Add up total points for this section:
_ _ _ _ _ = Total points for this section

Divided by: _ _ _ _ _ _ (number of statements answered) = _ _ _ _ _ _
Average score for this section

Transfer your score to the Chief Revenue Officer Index at the beginning of the

Self-Assessment.

CRITERION #4: ANALYZE:

INTENT: Analyze causes, assumptions and hypotheses.

In my belief, the answer to this question is clearly defined:

5 Strongly Agree

4 Agree

3 Neutral

2 Disagree

1 Strongly Disagree

1. What does the data say about the performance of the stakeholder process?
<--- Score

2. What were the financial benefits resulting from any 'ground fruit or low-hanging fruit' (quick fixes)?
<--- Score

3. Was a detailed process map created to amplify critical steps of the 'as is' stakeholder process?

<--- Score

4. Were Pareto charts (or similar) used to portray the 'heavy hitters' (or key sources of variation)?
<--- Score

5. How can data science be used to optimize decision making in organizations?
<--- Score

6. How often will devices send data to the cloud?
<--- Score

7. What have various industries experienced with inadvertent leaks or intentional hacking of confidential data?
<--- Score

8. Are gaps between current performance and the goal performance identified?
<--- Score

9. What did the team gain from developing a sub-process map?
<--- Score

10. Where is the data coming from to measure compliance?
<--- Score

11. How have you or your team tried to aggregate data from disparate systems to create a single source of truth?
<--- Score

12. What is the complexity of the output produced?

<--- Score

13. What data do you need to collect?
<--- Score

14. Is the performance gap determined?
<--- Score

15. What programs/processes/approaches are needed to enable connections?
<--- Score

16. What would you do with the largest database of SaaS user data at your fingertips?
<--- Score

17. What are your outputs?
<--- Score

18. What kinds of data belong in the cloud?
<--- Score

19. Have the problem and goal statements been updated to reflect the additional knowledge gained from the analyze phase?
<--- Score

20. What is the cost of poor quality as supported by the team's analysis?
<--- Score

21. How is data used for program management and improvement?
<--- Score

22. What will drive Chief Revenue Officer change?

<--- Score

23. Does your current sales process have a clear Targeting Demand phase as to where and under what conditions Demand can be created?
<--- Score

24. How do you optimize the delivery of data science outcomes at the pace required by the business?
<--- Score

25. How are you transforming data into value to drive performance and growth for your organization?
<--- Score

26. What are your processes for onboarding new customers?
<--- Score

27. Do you trust the data of online research?
<--- Score

28. When should a process be art not science?
<--- Score

29. How has your approach to the media process changed as the marketing mix has fragmented across the media landscape?
<--- Score

30. How will corresponding data be collected?
<--- Score

31. What systems/processes must you excel at?

<--- Score

32. Does your organization have any preferred qualifications in mind for prospective employees?
<--- Score

33. What will the role of your Sales Operations team be to drive and support sales strategy and technology?
<--- Score

34. Did any additional data need to be collected?
<--- Score

35. Is your cloud prepared to receive the amount of data that will return?
<--- Score

36. What are the Chief Revenue Officer design outputs?
<--- Score

37. How do software improvements drive physical security?
<--- Score

38. What is the biggest risk to data availability in the businesses you see?
<--- Score

39. Where are the opportunities to align and mutually benefit?
<--- Score

40. Does your current sales process have a clear Creating Demand phase?

<--- Score

41. Who is involved with workflow mapping?
<--- Score

42. Are corporations making the appropriate legal and ethical decisions about destroying data?
<--- Score

43. What tools were used to generate the list of possible causes?
<--- Score

44. What are the opportunities, the pros and cons?
<--- Score

45. What tools were used to narrow the list of possible causes?
<--- Score

46. Were there any improvement opportunities identified from the process analysis?
<--- Score

47. Is there any way to speed up the process?
<--- Score

48. Where do you see the most opportunity and why?
<--- Score

49. What training opportunities have you taken advantage of and why?
<--- Score

50. Which of your existing data sources will be

most valuable for API-driven applications?
<--- Score

51. What do you believe sales teams should do to address lingering issues with onboarding processes?
<--- Score

52. How do you use data to profit in the future?
<--- Score

53. How many input/output points does it require?
<--- Score

54. How adequate is the data that you receive?
<--- Score

55. Is pre-qualification of suppliers carried out?
<--- Score

56. How else are finance teams aggregating data from disparate systems?
<--- Score

57. What is the process for setting performance goals?
<--- Score

58. What are the compelling events that drive sales?
<--- Score

59. How can partners truly monetize big data?
<--- Score

60. How can finance executives transform data

into actionable insights?
<--- Score

61. Is there anything structural about it that would prevent it from being a tremendous revenue opportunity for you as well going forward?
<--- Score

62. What opportunity for profit or risk of loss is there for the worker?
<--- Score

63. How successful are teams in integrating the data?
<--- Score

64. Is one over-investing in unqualified opportunities?
<--- Score

65. When was your sales process installed?
<--- Score

66. How was the detailed process map generated, verified, and validated?
<--- Score

67. Did any value-added analysis or 'lean thinking' take place to identify some of the gaps shown on the 'as is' process map?
<--- Score

68. Is the Chief Revenue Officer process severely broken such that a re-design is necessary?
<--- Score

69. What were the crucial 'moments of truth' on the process map?
<--- Score

70. Does your current sales process have a clear Shaping Demand phase?
<--- Score

71. Does your current sales process involve methods for providing business development personnel with Thought Leadership necessary for Targeting, Creating, and Shaping Demand?
<--- Score

72. How do digital technologies drive economic growth?
<--- Score

73. How does the organization define, manage, and improve its Chief Revenue Officer processes?
<--- Score

74. What factors drive your level of involvement in types of projects?
<--- Score

75. What are your Chief Revenue Officer processes?
<--- Score

76. How is the way you as the leader think and process information affecting your organizational culture?
<--- Score

77. Who will facilitate the team and process?
<--- Score

78. How does the board of directors oversee your risk management process?

<--- Score

79. How do you use Chief Revenue Officer data and information to support organizational decision making and innovation?

<--- Score

80. What are the opportunities and risks surrounding an investment into the cloud?

<--- Score

81. What conclusions were drawn from the team's data collection and analysis? How did the team reach these conclusions?

<--- Score

82. What Chief Revenue Officer data should be managed?

<--- Score

83. Are all staff in core Chief Revenue Officer subjects Highly Qualified?

<--- Score

84. Is data and process analysis, root cause analysis and quantifying the gap/opportunity in place?

<--- Score

85. Why should your organizations access to compensation data be any different?

<--- Score

86. What are the processes for audit reporting and management?

<--- Score

87. What other jobs or tasks affect the performance of the steps in the Chief Revenue Officer process?
<--- Score

88. What are the revised rough estimates of the financial savings/opportunity for Chief Revenue Officer improvements?
<--- Score

89. Does it still help close sales opportunities?
<--- Score

90. Do you share data with other firms?
<--- Score

91. What are the barriers that may prevent your organization from participating in the procurement process?
<--- Score

92. What quality tools were used to get through the analyze phase?
<--- Score

93. What Chief Revenue Officer metrics are outputs of the process?
<--- Score

94. Is the gap/opportunity displayed and communicated in financial terms?
<--- Score

95. Does your current sales process deploy tools, methods and techniques for Targeting, Creating

and Shaping Demand?
<--- Score

96. How do marketers leverage data to improve performance?
<--- Score

97. How will the data be checked for quality?
<--- Score

98. Have any additional benefits been identified that will result from closing all or most of the gaps?
<--- Score

99. What is the Value Stream Mapping?
<--- Score

100. How robust are the processes in place to test for efficiency and make efficiency improvements?
<--- Score

101. How do see opportunities and react faster?
<--- Score

102. How do you know your data is secure?
<--- Score

103. What Chief Revenue Officer data will be collected?
<--- Score

104. Were any designed experiments used to generate additional insight into the data analysis?
<--- Score

105. What are the disruptive Chief Revenue Officer

technologies that enable your organization to radically change your business processes?
<--- Score

106. Is your business process easy and effective?
<--- Score

107. Which tools and data are being used to manage reporting?
<--- Score

108. How would you characterize your data management function in terms of importance and maturity?
<--- Score

109. How important is it to have an established process and strategy to improve sales performance?
<--- Score

110. Was a cause-and-effect diagram used to explore the different types of causes (or sources of variation)?
<--- Score

111. How do you use data to pro fit in the future?
<--- Score

Add up total points for this section:
_ _ _ _ _ = Total points for this section

Divided by: _ _ _ _ _ _ (number of statements answered) = _ _ _ _ _ _
Average score for this section

Transfer your score to the Chief Revenue

Officer Index at the beginning of the
Self-Assessment.

CRITERION #5: IMPROVE:

INTENT: Develop a practical solution.
Innovate, establish and test the
solution and to measure the results.

In my belief, the answer to this
question is clearly defined:

5 Strongly Agree

4 Agree

3 Neutral

2 Disagree

1 Strongly Disagree

**1. How open are you about giving the
development team a voice?**
<--- Score

2. What tools were used to tap into the creativity and
encourage 'outside the box' thinking?
<--- Score

3. What is Chief Revenue Officer's impact on utilizing

the best solution(s)?
<--- Score

4. How does sales operations work to improve sales productivity and effectiveness without becoming the dumping ground for any task that sits outside of the core selling roles?
<--- Score

5. Who knows enough about the business to know where all the inherent risk lies?
<--- Score

6. What practices helps your organization to develop its capacity to recognize patterns?
<--- Score

7. Is there any understanding among the manufacturers to regulate prices?
<--- Score

8. Are there smaller P&Ls within your organization that can serve as great training grounds for leaders to develop solid business-management skills?
<--- Score

9. What are the top areas in which you need to develop skills?
<--- Score

10. What alternative responses are available to manage risk?
<--- Score

11. How does employee engagement play into risk

management?
<--- Score

12. Is it worth the time savings to improve?
<--- Score

13. What metrics should CEOs follow to improve sales and marketing alignment?
<--- Score

14. How do you encourage more private sector development?
<--- Score

15. Is the Chief Revenue Officer solution sustainable?
<--- Score

16. What is the team's contingency plan for potential problems occurring in implementation?
<--- Score

17. What are the strategies to better manage the risk of Botrytis bunch rot?
<--- Score

18. Is there a cost/benefit analysis of optimal solution(s)?
<--- Score

19. Are you aware of the risks concerning Internal Audit today and in the near future?
<--- Score

20. What are the behaviors that signal imminent insider risk or vulnerability?
<--- Score

21. What is the implementation plan?
<--- Score

22. What is the most difficult business decision you have had to make?
<--- Score

23. Was a pilot designed for the proposed solution(s)?
<--- Score

24. Are the most efficient solutions problem-specific?
<--- Score

25. Where is your organization in development?
<--- Score

26. Does leveraging outsourced franchise development make sense for your brand?
<--- Score

27. Have you considered what is a fair allocation of risk with your counterparties?
<--- Score

28. Is the optimal solution selected based on testing and analysis?
<--- Score

29. What is risk and why is risk so often viewed in negative terms?
<--- Score

30. What are the key risks of investing in your organization?
<--- Score

31. How is it being measured, what are the results?
<--- Score

32. What are the Chief Revenue Officer security risks?
<--- Score

33. Were any criteria developed to assist the team in testing and evaluating potential solutions?
<--- Score

34. Is the implementation plan designed?
<--- Score

35. Is there any other Chief Revenue Officer solution?
<--- Score

36. Are the key business and technology risks being managed?
<--- Score

37. What communications are necessary to support the implementation of the solution?
<--- Score

38. Does your marketing department provide business improvement value propositions for sales professionals to utilize in demand creation activities?
<--- Score

39. Do you have the optimal project management team structure?
<--- Score

40. What can businesses do to optimize talent and

human capital?

<--- Score

41. What is the optimal marketing strategy?

<--- Score

42. What attendant changes will need to be made to ensure that the solution is successful?

<--- Score

43. Is there a high likelihood that any recommendations will achieve their intended results?

<--- Score

44. What are the benefits of pursuing enterprise risk management?

<--- Score

45. Are the risks fully understood, reasonable and manageable?

<--- Score

46. Is there a small-scale pilot for proposed improvement(s)? What conclusions were drawn from the outcomes of a pilot?

<--- Score

47. What are the most ambitious results you can achieve down to the least?

<--- Score

48. What does it take to optimize digital Customer Experience?

<--- Score

49. What or who is a chief operating decision

maker?
<--- Score

50. Is a contingency plan established?
<--- Score

51. What creative innovations are driving results?
<--- Score

52. What if you had an archiving solution with the power to unlock that value?
<--- Score

53. What are some of your favorite rep development tactics?
<--- Score

54. Who manages supplier risk management in your organization?
<--- Score

55. What tools were used to evaluate the potential solutions?
<--- Score

56. How did the team generate the list of possible solutions?
<--- Score

57. What is Chief Revenue Officer risk?
<--- Score

58. Who will be responsible for documenting the Chief Revenue Officer requirements in detail?
<--- Score

59. Who are the Chief Revenue Officer decision makers?
<--- Score

60. What value and results do connected marketing/sales/service functions enable?
<--- Score

61. Risk events: what are the things that could go wrong?
<--- Score

62. How does the technology provide a solution?
<--- Score

63. Are there any constraints (technical, political, cultural, or otherwise) that would inhibit certain solutions?
<--- Score

64. What is your single largest security risk?
<--- Score

65. Has your team been able to translate customer engagement into tangible results?
<--- Score

66. How will the group know that the solution worked?
<--- Score

67. Have the main strategic risks to the program been identified?
<--- Score

68. How well has your organization developed

strong knowledge and skills in each digital marketing strategy area?

<--- Score

69. Describe the design of the pilot and what tests were conducted, if any?

<--- Score

70. How should security risks and challenges be addressed?

<--- Score

71. What are the risks to your business?

<--- Score

72. How can SaaS marketers better improve and personalize marketing?

<--- Score

73. How often does your organization perform an assessment of high-risk third parties?

<--- Score

74. How is continuous improvement applied to risk management?

<--- Score

75. How are you mitigating risk and exploiting the competitive advantage for your customer base?

<--- Score

76. Are new and improved process ('should be') maps developed?

<--- Score

77. Do you understand why your customers buy

your solution?
<--- Score

78. Do you have access to the decision makers in the customer organization?
<--- Score

79. How can you better manage risk?
<--- Score

80. Does the limited risk sharing arrangement make the Eurozone more fragile?
<--- Score

81. How will the team or the process owner(s) monitor the implementation plan to see that it is working as intended?
<--- Score

82. What tools were most useful during the improve phase?
<--- Score

83. Is pilot data collected and analyzed?
<--- Score

84. What are the generic actions that can be defined as insider risk?
<--- Score

85. What do you do to improve your business acumen to prepare for leadership?
<--- Score

86. Have you identified breakpoints and/or risk tolerances that will trigger broad consideration of

a potential need for intervention or modification of strategy?

<--- Score

87. What error proofing will be done to address some of the discrepancies observed in the 'as is' process?

<--- Score

88. Can you identify any significant risks or exposures to Chief Revenue Officer third- parties (vendors, service providers, alliance partners etc) that concern you?

<--- Score

89. Which Chief Revenue Officer solution is appropriate?

<--- Score

90. Do the results match up with your marketing strategy for the year?

<--- Score

91. Are the best solutions selected?

<--- Score

92. How can finance mitigate risk from human behavior that runs counter to corporate goals and overall strategy?

<--- Score

93. Is the scope clearly documented?

<--- Score

94. Do you have a strong knowledge and understanding of marketing and sales strategies?

<--- Score

95. What assumptions are made about the solution and approach?
<--- Score

96. What are the top areas in which you need to develop skills in your marketing organization?
<--- Score

97. Does your organization value continuous quality improvement and knowledge management?
<--- Score

98. Can you integrate quality management and risk management?
<--- Score

99. Are risk management tasks balanced centrally and locally?
<--- Score

100. How will you recognize and celebrate results?
<--- Score

101. What is the risk of identity theft?
<--- Score

102. How does the solution remove the key sources of issues discovered in the analyze phase?
<--- Score

103. Do you understand how your customers and prospects make purchase decisions?
<--- Score

104. Do other forms of management guidance improve forecast accuracy?

<--- Score

105. What can you do to improve?

<--- Score

106. Who are the Chief Revenue Officer decision-makers?

<--- Score

107. What lessons, if any, from a pilot were incorporated into the design of the full-scale solution?

<--- Score

108. What were the underlying assumptions on the cost-benefit analysis?

<--- Score

109. How does risk fit into the expanded role of the CFO?

<--- Score

110. What are your current levels and trends in key measures or indicators of workforce and leader development?

<--- Score

111. Are procedures documented for managing Chief Revenue Officer risks?

<--- Score

112. Is a solution implementation plan established, including schedule/work breakdown structure, resources, risk management plan, cost/budget, and control plan?

<--- Score

113. Are possible solutions generated and tested?
<--- Score

114. Are events managed to resolution?
<--- Score

115. What are the required risk areas for an effective compliance program?
<--- Score

116. Are improved process ('should be') maps modified based on pilot data and analysis?
<--- Score

117. What teams/key executives are CFOs collaborating with closely to minimize risk?
<--- Score

118. How do you optimize digital customer experience?
<--- Score

119. How does your organization contribute to the development of the industry or individual firms?
<--- Score

120. How does risk intelligent compliance fit into the risk intelligent enterprise as a whole?
<--- Score

121. Is Chief Revenue Officer documentation maintained?
<--- Score

122. What does the 'should be' process map/design look like?
<--- Score

123. How is knowledge sharing about risk management improved?
<--- Score

124. Are organizational investors part of the problem or part of the solution?
<--- Score

125. How do you keep improving Chief Revenue Officer?
<--- Score

126. What are the recent trends and developments in the niche?
<--- Score

Add up total points for this section:
_ _ _ _ _ = Total points for this section

Divided by: _ _ _ _ _ _ (number of statements answered) = _ _ _ _ _ _
Average score for this section

Transfer your score to the Chief Revenue Officer Index at the beginning of the Self-Assessment.

CRITERION #6: CONTROL:

INTENT: Implement the practical solution. Maintain the performance and correct possible complications.

In my belief, the answer to this question is clearly defined:

5 Strongly Agree

4 Agree

3 Neutral

2 Disagree

1 Strongly Disagree

1. How is change control managed?
<--- Score

2. Who is the Chief Revenue Officer process owner?
<--- Score

3. How can machine learning be leveraged to create predictive insights?
<--- Score

4. What are the key challenges that you have encounter with regards to anticipating and planning for risk?
<--- Score

5. What are the key controls for securing IIoT devices?
<--- Score

6. How will innovation achieve scale?
<--- Score

7. How does your business effectively plan, execute and quantify the cost/benefit of a social media strategy?
<--- Score

8. What should the next improvement project be that is related to Chief Revenue Officer?
<--- Score

9. How much are you going to spend and where will spend it in order to execute your plan?
<--- Score

10. How will new or emerging customer needs/ requirements be checked/communicated to orient the process toward meeting the new specifications and continually reducing variation?
<--- Score

11. How will the day-to-day responsibilities for monitoring and continual improvement be transferred from the improvement team to the process owner?

<--- Score

12. Is a response plan established and deployed?
<--- Score

13. Do your investments reflect your growth agenda?
<--- Score

14. Does the Chief Revenue Officer performance meet the customer's requirements?
<--- Score

15. How do you plan to detect false disclosure information and enforce your policies?
<--- Score

16. How do larger, enterprise scale companies deal with the conflicting needs of Chief Financial Officers and Chief Revenue Officers and/or VPs of Sales?
<--- Score

17. What key inputs and outputs are being measured on an ongoing basis?
<--- Score

18. Do you monitor your network security today?
<--- Score

19. What is the recommended frequency of auditing?
<--- Score

20. What Chief Revenue Officer standards are applicable?
<--- Score

21. Is there a control plan in place for sustaining improvements (short and long-term)?
<--- Score

22. How will report readings be checked to effectively monitor performance?
<--- Score

23. Is there documentation that will support the successful operation of the improvement?
<--- Score

24. What quality tools were useful in the control phase?
<--- Score

25. How will the process owner and team be able to hold the gains?
<--- Score

26. Does the response plan contain a definite closed loop continual improvement scheme (e.g., plan-do-check-act)?
<--- Score

27. Is there an action plan in case of emergencies?
<--- Score

28. Have new or revised work instructions resulted?
<--- Score

29. Is there a documented and implemented monitoring plan?
<--- Score

30. Implementation Planning: is a pilot needed to test the changes before a full roll out occurs?
<--- Score

31. What other systems, operations, processes, and infrastructures (hiring practices, staffing, training, incentives/rewards, metrics/dashboards/scorecards, etc.) need updates, additions, changes, or deletions in order to facilitate knowledge transfer and improvements?
<--- Score

32. Which groups are involved in the sales planning process?
<--- Score

33. Does rising ceo pay simply reflect the market for skills?
<--- Score

34. How many iterations does your sales plan go through before it is finalized?
<--- Score

35. Is knowledge gained on process shared and institutionalized?
<--- Score

36. Are there other groups you would like to be involved in the sales planning process?
<--- Score

37. Has the improved process and its steps been standardized?
<--- Score

38. Why do you need the Standards of Business Conduct?

<--- Score

39. Do stock prices fully reflect information in accruals and cash flows about future earnings?

<--- Score

40. Do you monitor the Chief Revenue Officer decisions made and fine tune them as they evolve?

<--- Score

41. Are new process steps, standards, and documentation ingrained into normal operations?

<--- Score

42. What is your plan to assess your security risks?

<--- Score

43. Are documented procedures clear and easy to follow for the operators?

<--- Score

44. Will your organization utilize any conversion system when grading plans/exhibits?

<--- Score

45. How much do you plan to offer as an annual bonus?

<--- Score

46. Is new knowledge gained imbedded in the response plan?

<--- Score

47. How does does plan mesh with the markets?

<--- Score

48. What is the learning organization?
<--- Score

49. Do you really need to reshape a relationship (or a concept) so that it fits with your plans?
<--- Score

50. Do the viable solutions scale to future needs?
<--- Score

51. Do you monitor the effectiveness of your Chief Revenue Officer activities?
<--- Score

52. Does job training on the documented procedures need to be part of the process team's education and training?
<--- Score

53. Are there documented procedures?
<--- Score

54. How will the process owner verify improvement in present and future sigma levels, process capabilities?
<--- Score

55. What is your future proof technology plan?
<--- Score

56. What is the control/monitoring plan?
<--- Score

57. How far in advance do you typically plan activities for yourself and your employees?

<--- Score

58. Does a troubleshooting guide exist or is it needed?
<--- Score

59. Does it facilitate remote patient monitoring that meets requirements for billing?
<--- Score

60. How widespread is its use?
<--- Score

61. How do you plan for the cost of succession?
<--- Score

62. Are pertinent alerts monitored, analyzed and distributed to appropriate personnel?
<--- Score

63. What are the performance and scale of the Chief Revenue Officer tools?
<--- Score

64. What are the critical parameters to watch?
<--- Score

65. Who is going to spread your message?
<--- Score

66. How do your controls stack up?
<--- Score

67. Are suggested corrective/restorative actions indicated on the response plan for known causes to problems that might surface?
<--- Score

68. Is there a standardized process?
<--- Score

69. Are you thinking about a succession plan?
<--- Score

70. How many years worth of sales performance data is currently used in the planning process?
<--- Score

71. How will input, process, and output variables be checked to detect for sub-optimal conditions?
<--- Score

72. How can machine learning and AI help optimize the utilization of well site data?
<--- Score

73. What role do you play in the planning and oversight of large, critical projects?
<--- Score

74. How useless is the time off plan , really?
<--- Score

75. Are operating procedures consistent?
<--- Score

76. How is the internal audit plan developed?
<--- Score

77. How do you introduce and optimize data science and machine learning capabilities for analytics solutions?
<--- Score

78. Is reporting being used or needed?
<--- Score

79. What other areas of the group might benefit from the Chief Revenue Officer team's improvements, knowledge, and learning?
<--- Score

80. What can economists learn from happiness research?
<--- Score

81. How do you plan for performance improvements?
<--- Score

82. What direct to consumer market opportunities exist for medical device and monitoring companies?
<--- Score

83. Which, if any steps have you already taken/ plan to take to improve brand safety of your digital media buys?
<--- Score

84. Is there a recommended audit plan for routine surveillance inspections of Chief Revenue Officer's gains?
<--- Score

85. How much control do customers really want over interactions with a brand?
<--- Score

86. How might the group capture best practices and lessons learned so as to leverage improvements?
<--- Score

87. Is there a transfer of ownership and knowledge to process owner and process team tasked with the responsibilities.
<--- Score

88. Is a response plan in place for when the input, process, or output measures indicate an 'out-of-control' condition?
<--- Score

89. Will any special training be provided for results interpretation?
<--- Score

90. How is the sales compensation plan?
<--- Score

91. How is your client communicating changes to your organizations standard operating procedures?
<--- Score

Add up total points for this section:
_ _ _ _ _ = Total points for this section

Divided by: _ _ _ _ _ _ (number of statements answered) = _ _ _ _ _ _
Average score for this section

Transfer your score to the Chief Revenue Officer Index at the beginning of the Self-Assessment.

CRITERION #7: SUSTAIN:

INTENT: Retain the benefits.

In my belief, the answer to this question is clearly defined:

5 Strongly Agree

4 Agree

3 Neutral

2 Disagree

1 Strongly Disagree

1. Is the list of subsidiaries, as assembled by the Office of your organization Comptroller, correct?
<--- Score

2. What is customer centric marketing?
<--- Score

3. Are you losing market share to products from new categories?
<--- Score

4. Why is the establishment of compliance program beneficial?
<--- Score

5. What information do you consider in your review?
<--- Score

6. How do investigators get information from foreign sources?
<--- Score

7. What are the challenges you face in your role?
<--- Score

8. How are you going to grow the business?
<--- Score

9. Have you conducted any studies of how false content performs on your services?
<--- Score

10. What are the owners responsibilities?
<--- Score

11. How effective are your sales enablement tools?
<--- Score

12. Do you share details about the competitors sales strategy with members of your group?
<--- Score

13. How many boxes does your SaaS business tick?
<--- Score

14. What other key executive functions are you

collaborating most closely with?
<--- Score

15. How can behavioral patterns complement existing defences like Splunk and dark trace?
<--- Score

16. Is there duplication of activities across your organization?
<--- Score

17. What is a typical organizational structure for diversity and inclusion leadership?
<--- Score

18. What can all employees do to support the customer experience?
<--- Score

19. How does it relate to sales enablement?
<--- Score

20. Is having a mentor an essential part of getting ahead in a career?
<--- Score

21. Has the board adopted a code of ethics for board members and staff?
<--- Score

22. How well do you leverage technology?
<--- Score

23. What are your policies and procedures for related party transactions?
<--- Score

24. What challenges do you face with securing your IT infrastructure?

<--- Score

25. What are the key strengths and competitive advantages of your organization?

<--- Score

26. Do you know who your best customers are?

<--- Score

27. How important do you feel that is for the long-term success of a sales team?

<--- Score

28. What are the hot topics for you in Product, Subscription and Services Selling?

<--- Score

29. What initially attracted you to the enterprise SaaS space?

<--- Score

30. What is your organizations market share as a customer?

<--- Score

31. Do you use your block time effectively?

<--- Score

32. Have you always aspired to become a senior leader in technology?

<--- Score

33. Who has primary responsibility in your

organization for customer retention?
<--- Score

34. What is the most often cited reason for sales headcount voluntarily leaving your organization?
<--- Score

35. How else do you ensure that marketing provides sales with a consistent quantity and quality of leads?
<--- Score

36. What information should a board demand?
<--- Score

37. How much of your annual revenue do you estimate is attributable to inauthentic or false content?
<--- Score

38. What role do you usually take in a group meeting or consideration?
<--- Score

39. How important is it to be exposed to all areas of the business?
<--- Score

40. How do you see your responsibilities as a group member?
<--- Score

41. Do you sell on the time-payment business?
<--- Score

42. What are some best practices evidenced by

leading CEOs and companies?

<--- Score

43. Has there been any consolidation in the market in the number of suppliers (horizontal integration)?

<--- Score

44. What does it take to be a leader in the fast changing business of information technology?

<--- Score

45. How do business partners do less and give the business back more?

<--- Score

46. What are the duties of an Officer of a corporation and what are the potential penalties?

<--- Score

47. What is the market that you can realistically expand at a decent margin?

<--- Score

48. Do you prefer to work independently or on a team?

<--- Score

49. What makes practice partners different?

<--- Score

50. How is digital affecting the CMOs agenda?

<--- Score

51. Is the dispenser allowed to give away any samples for marketing purposes if the recipient is

eligible?
<--- Score

52. What type of search or rescue functions does your organization undertake?
<--- Score

53. Are you in the technology business or the customer service business?
<--- Score

54. Are there dominant suppliers, or is the market evenly distributed (market concentration)?
<--- Score

55. Which elements are included in your content marketing strategy?
<--- Score

56. Are there formal metrics in place for measuring and rewarding performance over time?
<--- Score

57. Will there be any other items of business on the agenda?
<--- Score

58. Which are your primary customers?
<--- Score

59. What is the difference between a leader and a manager?
<--- Score

60. Can the person or team execute well?
<--- Score

61. How are the KPIs used to present information?

<--- Score

62. What do you bring to customers that competitors can t?

<--- Score

63. Does the internal audit function get appropriate support from the CEO and senior management team?

<--- Score

64. Is there an industry wide culture clash between the IT centric nature of cloud systems and the physical security market?

<--- Score

65. Has the internal revenue service made any changes in taxable income?

<--- Score

66. Are your financial and human capital investments future proof?

<--- Score

67. What is the sweet spot of your channel in terms of target customer size?

<--- Score

68. How should your organizational structure change to meet new challenges?

<--- Score

69. How can airports work effectively with airlines to facilitate growth?

<--- Score

70. What is the culture of your business?
<--- Score

71. How effective is central organization forward guidance?
<--- Score

72. Do you know how effective your marketing campaigns are?
<--- Score

73. What information is already accessible?
<--- Score

74. Does your organization have a content marketing strategy?
<--- Score

75. What are you going to do about revenue?
<--- Score

76. How do you strike the balance between work and family?
<--- Score

77. What makes a great sales leader?
<--- Score

78. Which information do you use to present your set of KPIs?
<--- Score

79. What does your role involve in terms of helping your clients?

<--- Score

80. What do people value in politics?
<--- Score

81. Why dilute the total customer experience?
<--- Score

82. Is the airline industry model overall fixed?
<--- Score

83. What personal qualities should a leader have?
<--- Score

84. How do you use information to effect change?
<--- Score

85. How do you know where your business is in that range?
<--- Score

86. How do you know what customers want?
<--- Score

87. Who are the significant market participants, in terms of buyers, suppliers and the supply chain?
<--- Score

88. Are there any specific numbers or metrics you aim for to know if something is successful?
<--- Score

89. What is the relationship of the value cycle in detecting and limiting the liability of newness?
<--- Score

90. Is the current operation experiencing increases, decreases or at growth in customers?
<--- Score

91. Where do you find Revenue Marketers?
<--- Score

92. Is your innovation additive rather than disruptive?
<--- Score

93. Is organization distinctive strategy clearly articulated?
<--- Score

94. Is the desired outcome likely to involve significant business change?
<--- Score

95. What is your concept of the chief value of recreation?
<--- Score

96. What new salespeople want to know is, What do you do?
<--- Score

97. How will the growth of social media advertising affect your sales strategy?
<--- Score

98. Does your organization have other functions besides search or rescue?
<--- Score

99. How do you onboard your new salespeople?

<--- Score

100. Do you peer into the future and see SLAs leaders of tomorrow?
<--- Score

101. How do core beliefs about work affect worker engagement and organizational success?
<--- Score

102. Has the board adopted a conditional/ additional compensation policy governing all employees?
<--- Score

103. Who digs in and challenges the assumptions in your strategy?
<--- Score

104. How do you see that affecting the fundamental nature of marketing?
<--- Score

105. Is message consistent with how you brand your organization and position offers?
<--- Score

106. What are the methods a sustainability officer can use to further integrate sustainability into your organizations business operations when the officer has no ability to mandate that it be done?
<--- Score

107. How frequently do you receive user reports about inauthentic accounts?
<--- Score

108. What are the core skills and perspective that a stakeholder can bring to the business?
<--- Score

109. Does the division intend to score applications based on compliance with forthcoming rules as well as the act?
<--- Score

110. Do you promote your business online?
<--- Score

111. Do marketing and sales review wins and losses?
<--- Score

112. How can content strategy support them better?
<--- Score

113. How do you conduct your full-team meetings?
<--- Score

114. What is resonating with customers?
<--- Score

115. Have you had mentors through your career?
<--- Score

116. How has digital transformed the way in which CMOs structure teams?
<--- Score

117. How often is the Chief Executives appraisal administered?

<--- Score

118. What does a better practice revenue and rating strategy look like?
<--- Score

119. What are the important qualities a person should have to become an effective team member?
<--- Score

120. Are your marketing efforts strategically aligned to ensure business success?
<--- Score

121. How can consumer electronics companies incorporate product stewardship into business models?
<--- Score

122. What is the one thing you have to have to be a senior leader in IT?
<--- Score

123. What is the best profile of a sales person to hire into your organization?
<--- Score

124. Have recruiting and retaining strategies been inappropriate?
<--- Score

125. How many projects do you handle at a time?
<--- Score

126. Is it more effective to adapt the culture of your organization to its sustainability strategy

or try to integrate sustainability into your organizations culture?

<--- Score

127. Why should a customer pay for services?

<--- Score

128. What are the revenue strategies most likely to succeed in the coming years?

<--- Score

129. How interconnected should your Sales and Marketing teams be?

<--- Score

130. How can customers place orders with your organization?

<--- Score

131. How do your ideas move over time?

<--- Score

132. Is customer success fully formed at your organization?

<--- Score

133. Do happy employees report greater engagement and effort at work?

<--- Score

134. How do you ensure that email continues to evolve while juggling new marketing channels?

<--- Score

135. Have you sold or closed your business?

<--- Score

136. Which function in your organization is responsible for the customer experience today?
<--- Score

137. What is transformative technology, and how is it changing the way you work?
<--- Score

138. Why should a customer get services from you?
<--- Score

139. When is the right time to add a new position?
<--- Score

140. What are the key terms associated with money laundering?
<--- Score

141. What about discipline or rehabilitation for employees who test positive?
<--- Score

142. What is the most often cited reason for sales headcount involuntarily leaving your organization?
<--- Score

143. Do marketing and sales work together?
<--- Score

144. Are best practices shared across your organization?
<--- Score

145. What role does leadership play for a

supervisor or manager?

<--- Score

146. Have you experienced an overall productivity benefit since using cloud technology?

<--- Score

147. What are the critical moments in your customer journey?

<--- Score

148. What is the experience you want to create for customers?

<--- Score

149. Do your salespeople have tailor head-winds to success?

<--- Score

150. Does the real benefit lie in leveraging real-time payments?

<--- Score

151. How effective is your content marketing strategy compared with one year ago?

<--- Score

152. How does the Board recommend that you vote?

<--- Score

153. Do you enable single-sign-on with other cloud based SaaS services?

<--- Score

154. Which companies in your space are thriving

and which are struggling?

<--- Score

155. What was the most outstanding characteristic of that team?

<--- Score

156. What information must be included?

<--- Score

157. How does digital experience vary across different user segments on your website?

<--- Score

158. What does your IT team struggle with day to day?

<--- Score

159. What are the characteristics of a successful team?

<--- Score

160. What is your business doing to create a better world?

<--- Score

161. How is your organization leveraging new channels to engage with customers more effectively?

<--- Score

162. Is there really a crevasse between technical and leadership?

<--- Score

163. What do you do to welcome and orient new

hires into your department or team?
<--- Score

164. How is sales operations perceived today, and how should it be perceived in the future?
<--- Score

165. Is the current operation experiencing increases, decreases or flat growth in customers?
<--- Score

166. What percentage of your overall business do online sales represent?
<--- Score

167. How do you hack your sales time to accelerate your own Race to Zero?
<--- Score

168. Are departments interested in your cross channel sale?
<--- Score

169. What are the fees for money laundering?
<--- Score

170. What criteria will be utilized to differentiate scores for establishing goals for diversity?
<--- Score

171. Where do sales professionals fit in going forward?
<--- Score

172. Who will be contributing to your growth – your customers?

<--- Score

173. How old is the financial history of the business?
<--- Score

174. How would you handle a work crew with poor work habits or a staff member with a negative attitude?
<--- Score

175. How frequently do you provide real-time alerts?
<--- Score

176. What percentage of your marketing budget is dedicated to online marketing?
<--- Score

177. What is marketing supposed to deliver to sales?
<--- Score

178. What is the one thing you have to have to be an industry leader?
<--- Score

179. Are KPIs more about tick-box compliance than value-added insight?
<--- Score

180. What makes sales contests fail or succeed?
<--- Score

181. Does your organization provide a platform for suppliers to increase sales to other customers?

<--- Score

182. Who are your customers?
<--- Score

183. How does a customer get help at the right technical level?
<--- Score

184. How do you ensure a successful partnership of marketing and sales?
<--- Score

185. How can strategy leaders and the leadership team make the role of the strategy leader more effective?
<--- Score

186. What do ceos look for in sustainability executives?
<--- Score

187. Is there a day or time that is convenient for you?
<--- Score

188. How do you transition from the baseline to the target?
<--- Score

189. What are key technology changes to be aware of?
<--- Score

190. How does the board determine which directors are considered independent?

<--- Score

191. Do you share common vocabulary and information?
<--- Score

192. Who is responsible for cybersecurity?
<--- Score

193. Does the person on the team with the experience and knowledge have to be a principal officer?
<--- Score

194. What information is reported on operating segments?
<--- Score

195. What does it take for principal officers to provide prospective employees with the necessary training?
<--- Score

196. Who is a local large landowner, or runs a big local business?
<--- Score

197. What is a Chief Revenue Officer (CRO)?
<--- Score

198. Is there one struggle you see SaaS companies habitually endure?
<--- Score

199. Are you in a new Golden Era with the advent of so many marketing technologies?

<--- Score

200. How do you evaluate a sales rep?
<--- Score

201. What areas are you contemplating to source for managed services in the next year?
<--- Score

202. Is there any near future possibility of a disruptive technology emerging in the storage space?
<--- Score

203. Will overall ad spend grow or decline?
<--- Score

204. Are there any dominant supplier(s) in the market?
<--- Score

205. What must be included in the request for a team?
<--- Score

206. What is sales readiness software?
<--- Score

207. How much flexibility does a public employer have with compensatory time policies?
<--- Score

208. What are the barriers to implementation and what can be done to overcome them?
<--- Score

209. Who was involved in the implementation?
<--- Score

210. Is the information listed in order of importance and relevance to the position?
<--- Score

211. How do you set Chief Revenue Officer stretch targets and how do you get people to not only participate in setting these stretch targets but also that they strive to achieve these?
<--- Score

212. How to get your sales and marketing teams to start working together?
<--- Score

213. Does your organization use small business vendors for direct services or as part of its supply chain?
<--- Score

214. Do contributors to the shared collection participate in (or benefit from) any related business arrangement?
<--- Score

215. How does your business dispense online as an entrepreneur?
<--- Score

216. Why did it seem that the emergency room staff was seeing the system for the first time?
<--- Score

217. What are the key factors transforming your

industry right now?

<--- Score

218. What does it take to become a Chief Information Officer?

<--- Score

219. How do your rate your knowledge of technology?

<--- Score

220. Is the chief audit executive respected within the auditing profession?

<--- Score

221. How do you respond to ongoing threat?

<--- Score

222. What are the large trends in terms of the large population, economy?

<--- Score

223. How many years should a professional maintain run-off cover?

<--- Score

224. How do you use social media to build a social selling machine?

<--- Score

225. Do you work better by yourself or as part of a team?

<--- Score

226. Which content marketing tactics does your organization use?

<--- Score

227. How to safely reward extra work by exempt salaried employees?
<--- Score

228. Are you seeing more intrusions or phishing attempts?
<--- Score

229. How many levels of management do you deal with?
<--- Score

230. Is the business model sustainable in the long term?
<--- Score

231. Do you have a strong bench of talent when it comes to CEO succession?
<--- Score

232. What changes do you make to the team to get the dashboards up?
<--- Score

233. Does the market have significant links to other markets?
<--- Score

234. Is your accounting system hampering growth?
<--- Score

235. Does your business have the capacity for additional customers?

<--- Score

236. How much of the news content that is shared on your services do you estimate is false?
<--- Score

237. Where do you see most content marketing strategies faltering?
<--- Score

238. What happens if additional items of business are presented at the Annual Meeting?
<--- Score

239. Do your incentives support customer centric behaviors?
<--- Score

240. Has the form ever engaged with its local workforce investment board?
<--- Score

241. Who is responsible for requesting a team?
<--- Score

242. Are there common officers and/or directors between you and the business?
<--- Score

243. What are your most prominent memories of your time there?
<--- Score

244. Which content marketing tools does your organization currently use?
<--- Score

245. Can stockholders and other interested parties communicate directly with the Board?

<--- Score

246. What kind of content and experiences will consumers demand?

<--- Score

247. Is the goal here to provide marketing materials to all customers at a range of touch points?

<--- Score

248. Is the management failing in some way?

<--- Score

249. How does good business partnering succeed?

<--- Score

250. How would the manufacturer get the advantage?

<--- Score

251. What is your position in your organization?

<--- Score

252. How would the service users respond to any price changes?

<--- Score

253. What is the Benefit of a Revenue Stack Audit?

<--- Score

254. Is the humanity adoption of technology what is changing the industry?

<--- Score

255. How effectively is social media linked to your organizations marketing strategy?
<--- Score

256. How important is CEO commitment?
<--- Score

257. What are your goals for your work together?
<--- Score

258. How do you track the effectiveness of your messaging?
<--- Score

259. What have various sectors of the industry had to do to prepare?
<--- Score

260. Is there misalignment, friction, or tension between your revenue and digital teams?
<--- Score

261. Will your organization provide you with a platform to achieve your personal goals?
<--- Score

262. How can business leaders prepare?
<--- Score

263. Can the division provide further details or examples of the types of relevant business transactions and financial information it is seeking with respect to addendum a?
<--- Score

264. How many shares must be present or represented to conduct business at the Annual Meeting?
<--- Score

265. How to get the most out of automation and employees?
<--- Score

266. What are the communications challenges your organization might face while promoting green initiatives?
<--- Score

267. How do you use customer objections in your marketing materials?
<--- Score

268. How is content marketing structured within your organization?
<--- Score

269. Do the bulk of your revenues come from legacy brands in shrinking or sluggish categories?
<--- Score

270. What resources will you put toward your goals?
<--- Score

271. Is there a timeline established for individuals granted licenses to be open or operating by?
<--- Score

272. Will your organization maintain its footing as

one of the powerful legacy airlines, or will it join the many ghosts of the airline industrys past?
<--- Score

273. What does it imply in terms of the asymmetry of information between your clients?
<--- Score

274. Are you elected by the public into your position or appointed by your organization?
<--- Score

275. What are your organizations sources of revenues?
<--- Score

276. What have you done organizationally to add accountability to the delivery of omnichannel?
<--- Score

277. Can private companies be forced to reveal private information concerning employees?
<--- Score

278. Does marketing sit in on sales calls?
<--- Score

279. Do you imagine a more supportive workplace?
<--- Score

280. How does that industry feel about technology?
<--- Score

281. How and when do you implement

vulnerability and system patches?

<--- Score

282. What does the blended store look like to your customer?

<--- Score

283. Has your sales manager ever gotten a standing ovation?

<--- Score

284. How to create customer facing and ecosystem facing IT services?

<--- Score

285. How have your partners incorporated security?

<--- Score

286. What stage are you in on your omnichannel journey?

<--- Score

287. What role does your IT department play with API-based applications?

<--- Score

288. What security markets are likely to embrace ai?

<--- Score

289. Which customers get what experience?

<--- Score

290. Are there specific technology stacks you should stay away from?

<--- Score

291. Are you kind of, nearly, almost there?
<--- Score

292. How important is coaching to a Sales teams success?
<--- Score

293. Does the board have a lead independent director?
<--- Score

294. How long does the average sale take?
<--- Score

295. Does the project have visibility & support from key executives?
<--- Score

296. What role are strategy leaders currently playing to help organizations navigate toward a changing future?
<--- Score

297. What are your goals and what will you do to meet?
<--- Score

298. What is the correct group of people for information to reach?
<--- Score

299. How is your organization addressing workforce diversity?
<--- Score

300. Will that lead to a net benefit either for them or for society?

<--- Score

301. What suppliers are leading the introduction of new technologies and products to market?

<--- Score

302. How do you keep up to date with changing technology?

<--- Score

303. What are some ways the project has helped you in your role?

<--- Score

304. Is there any restriction on the hours of operations?

<--- Score

305. How many employees are in your organization?

<--- Score

306. How do you upgrade core services or products?

<--- Score

307. How do you extend the value of IT beyond the provisioning of infrastructure and applications?

<--- Score

308. Does it help you and your customers accelerate your view of collaboration?

<--- Score

309. What are the benefits of a Chief Revenue Officer?

<--- Score

310. What was your percentage of ownership in the business?

<--- Score

311. What has been your favorite/least favorite position and why?

<--- Score

312. What are the responsibilities of the board of directors?

<--- Score

313. What is your organizations management style?

<--- Score

314. What do you consider to be the biggest challenges for a CMO days?

<--- Score

315. Do you harness technology in the service of your aspirations?

<--- Score

316. What is your background and how did you arrive at your current role?

<--- Score

317. What function of your organization do you work in?

<--- Score

318. How valuable are mentors, sponsors, and connectors for your career progression?

<--- Score

319. Have all board members been asked to contribute?

<--- Score

320. Is it time to abolish social media?

<--- Score

321. How many of the accounts on your service do you estimate are inauthentic?

<--- Score

322. What do prospects remember after you leave office?

<--- Score

323. Is your organization stating that shareholders, members, officers cannot lend financial resources if there is a cash flow shortage?

<--- Score

324. How does inbound marketing fit into the entire media mix of your organizations marketing?

<--- Score

325. Have you worked with a board before?

<--- Score

326. How would you rate your organizations marketing excellence?

<--- Score

327. Why do systems integrators continue installing insecure systems?

<--- Score

328. Does social selling supplement or replace traditional sales methods?

<--- Score

329. Why put all that time into creating visual systems?

<--- Score

330. Are there employees/contractors in the business?

<--- Score

331. What are the advantages, if any, of establishing team goals as opposed to individual goals?

<--- Score

332. How can the cloud help revolutionize the business in terms of increasing efficiency?

<--- Score

333. How are brands starting to think differently when it comes to engaging with customers?

<--- Score

334. Have you ever designed original graphics?

<--- Score

335. How did that first Board appointment come about?

<--- Score

336. What new and emerging technology platforms to use?

<--- Score

337. How has your role evolved over the past few years?

<--- Score

338. How is the marketing cycle changing over time for different leads or campaigns?

<--- Score

339. How do you package and sell your support?

<--- Score

340. Is the business reliant upon you?

<--- Score

341. What are the pricing or chargeback models for services?

<--- Score

342. Does placing marketing, sales and service under one senior leader enable a better customer experience?

<--- Score

343. Does technology motivate people to stay healthy?

<--- Score

344. What are the sources of that revenue?

<--- Score

345. What qualities and values does a leader have?

<--- Score

346. Are you, as a technical account manager, or a technical sales person, able to articulate the product value proposition to deal with that pain?
<--- Score

347. What to expect from its new media strategy?
<--- Score

348. How do you execute The Ultimate Sales Hack?
<--- Score

349. How do you look behind assurances?
<--- Score

350. Has your ideal customer has changed?
<--- Score

351. How do you navigate the various funding options for growth?
<--- Score

352. Are special items an earnings-management tool?
<--- Score

353. Who are the key management personnel of your organization?
<--- Score

354. How can companies better prepare sellers for a new role in serving customers?
<--- Score

355. What is the most rewarding part of your role at the moment?

<--- Score

356. How do you create buy-in?
<--- Score

357. What goals have you set for yourself?
<--- Score

358. What soft skills/characteristics are integral to the role?
<--- Score

359. Which formats and partnerships portend the best strategies for winning viewers and building sales?
<--- Score

360. What do you contribute to establish a positive working environment for your team?
<--- Score

361. Does the chief executive receive a performance appraisal?
<--- Score

362. What does today look like for your customers?
<--- Score

363. How do you expect Alignment in your organization without the right Tech enablement?
<--- Score

364. How can stockholders communicate with the board of directors?
<--- Score

365. Are your customers delighted by your services and products?

<--- Score

366. Has your organization already implemented?

<--- Score

367. How responsive is customer service?

<--- Score

368. How do you get electronic access to other related information?

<--- Score

369. What does that pattern do to your revenue?

<--- Score

370. How effectively is your organization delivering its core business?

<--- Score

371. How much is a SaaS business worth?

<--- Score

372. Do you get from the what of change management to the how?

<--- Score

373. How do you maximise your energy efficiency?

<--- Score

374. What is your businesss strategy?

<--- Score

375. Will you still be able to work with employees?

<--- Score

376. What does the business hope to achieve in the long term?

<--- Score

377. Are you tired of dealing with uneducated sales people?

<--- Score

378. When should the sales person go hunting for both value propositions?

<--- Score

379. When do you expect to make your first sale?

<--- Score

380. What transcendent KPIs should business units collaborate and align around?

<--- Score

381. Where does it make sense for your sales or success people to increase in-person visits?

<--- Score

382. How can organizations and strategy leaders stay ahead of it all?

<--- Score

383. Are suppliers dependent on other suppliers for key components?

<--- Score

384. How and when will the IT strategy become affected from the business strategic adjustments?

<--- Score

385. What experience do you have in project management field?

<--- Score

386. How do you factor in both for your short to medium term IT strategy?

<--- Score

387. Has the board adopted bylaws and made them available to board members and staff?

<--- Score

388. What are your principals for doing good business?

<--- Score

389. Where is there value in markets and how can investors unlock it?

<--- Score

390. How realistic is it for a small organization to use inbound marketing if the content creation demands are so high?

<--- Score

391. Can the dispensary be designed with tall and transparent windows in the front of the facility?

<--- Score

392. How does your organization generate its revenue?

<--- Score

393. Can technology change the world?

<--- Score

394. Are you truly fully formed customer success organizations today?

<--- Score

395. Why is the business an attractive proposition?

<--- Score

396. The political context: who holds power?

<--- Score

397. How does lead routing affect revenue?

<--- Score

398. How diverse are your business categories in terms of consumer base and channel?

<--- Score

399. What is your fundraising strategy?

<--- Score

400. When should you start marketing to generate leads?

<--- Score

401. Is a credit more effective at meeting its goals than a spending program would be?

<--- Score

402. Why are you blaming salespeople for missing quota?

<--- Score

403. What more could your organization want from a leader?

<--- Score

404. Have there been challenges in starting or expanding the business?

<--- Score

405. What soft skills are integral to the role?

<--- Score

406. What factors would you consider in assembling a project team?

<--- Score

407. Do you want a Builder or a Grower for the role?

<--- Score

408. How do you become a marketplace leader?

<--- Score

409. What about from the end user perspective?

<--- Score

410. How well has your organization articulated its purpose, vision and strategy to its staff and stakeholders?

<--- Score

411. What is a service provider to do?

<--- Score

412. How important is each channel your organization uses to its overall content marketing success?

<--- Score

413. What is the deal with sales talent today?

<--- Score

414. How do you change your approach to make the procurement more attractive?

<--- Score

415. Who is responsible for customer experience now?

<--- Score

416. Who provides money laundering services?

<--- Score

417. What are the various phases of diversity and inclusion leadership maturity?

<--- Score

418. Where does the business get customers from?

<--- Score

419. How will you ensure long-term success in your new role?

<--- Score

420. Is there a clear Performance Management & execution program?

<--- Score

421. What % could be considered successful and over what period of time?

<--- Score

422. How effective are your sales enablement programs?

<--- Score

423. What are the prospects for growth and

advancement?
<--- Score

424. How effective is your sales execution?
<--- Score

425. What is the best way to track conversions?
<--- Score

426. How would you rate your ability as a employee?
<--- Score

427. How is that possible if were applying for a first time conditional license?
<--- Score

428. How will wearables and IoT devices affect the way you consume, rest and play?
<--- Score

429. How will business models and value chain competition evolve?
<--- Score

430. What is your ideal customer size?
<--- Score

431. How does inbound marketing connect to sales?
<--- Score

432. What is your biggest challenge with respect to information security?
<--- Score

433. Does your organization receive, on the whole, positive word of mouth from its customers?
<--- Score

434. What is the hardest thing about being a leader?
<--- Score

435. How much of the activity on your service do you estimate is inauthentic or false?
<--- Score

436. What role do you play in ensuring a smooth working environment?
<--- Score

Add up total points for this section:
_____ = Total points for this section

Divided by: _____ (number of statements answered) = _____
Average score for this section

Transfer your score to the Chief Revenue Officer Index at the beginning of the Self-Assessment.

Chief Revenue Officer and Managing Projects, Criteria for Project Managers:

1.0 Initiating Process Group: Chief Revenue Officer

1. Establishment of pm office?

2. Will the Chief Revenue Officer project meet the client requirements, and will it achieve the business success criteria that justified doing the Chief Revenue Officer project in the first place?

3. What input will you be required to provide the Chief Revenue Officer project team?

4. At which stage, in a typical Chief Revenue Officer project do stake holders have maximum influence?

5. What were things that you did well, and could improve, and how?

6. What are the pressing issues of the hour?

7. Did you use a contractor or vendor?

8. Did the Chief Revenue Officer project team have the right skills?

9. Information sharing?

10. Based on your Chief Revenue Officer project communication management plan, what worked well?

11. Have the stakeholders identified all individual requirements pertaining to business process?

12. What are the tools and techniques to be used in each phase?

13. Were escalated issues resolved promptly?

14. Who is behind the Chief Revenue Officer project?

15. Do you know the Chief Revenue Officer projects goal, purpose and objectives?

16. What communication items need improvement?

17. What technical work to do in each phase?

18. Were decisions made in a timely manner?

19. At which cmmi level are software processes documented, standardized, and integrated into a standard to-be practiced process for your organization?

20. Are the Chief Revenue Officer project team and stakeholders meeting regularly and using a meeting agenda and taking notes to accurately document what is being covered and what happened in the weekly meetings?

1.1 Project Charter: Chief Revenue Officer

21. What is the justification?

22. Who will take notes, document decisions?

23. Where and how does the team fit within your organization structure?

24. Are there special technology requirements?

25. What does it need to do?

26. Did your Chief Revenue Officer project ask for this?

27. Must Have?

28. Why is a Chief Revenue Officer project Charter used?

29. Assumptions: what factors, for planning purposes, are you considering to be true?

30. How are Chief Revenue Officer projects different from operations?

31. What barriers do you predict to your success?

32. What outcome, in measureable terms, are you hoping to accomplish?

33. Who manages integration?

34. What are the constraints?

35. Chief Revenue Officer project deliverables: what is the Chief Revenue Officer project going to produce?

36. Why Outsource?

37. Why executive support?

38. What metrics could you look at?

39. Will this replace an existing product?

40. Pop quiz – which are the same inputs as in the Chief Revenue Officer project charter?

1.2 Stakeholder Register: Chief Revenue Officer

41. How much influence do they have on the Chief Revenue Officer project?

42. How will reports be created?

43. Who is managing stakeholder engagement?

44. How big is the gap?

45. What & Why?

46. What is the power of the stakeholder?

47. What opportunities exist to provide communications?

48. Who wants to talk about Security?

49. Who are the stakeholders?

50. What are the major Chief Revenue Officer project milestones requiring communications or providing communications opportunities?

51. Is your organization ready for change?

52. How should employers make voices heard?

1.3 Stakeholder Analysis Matrix: Chief Revenue Officer

53. What unique or lowest-cost resources does the Chief Revenue Officer project have access to?

54. What should thwe organizations stakeholders avoid?

55. How does the Chief Revenue Officer project involve consultations or collaboration with other organizations?

56. Who is most dependent on the resources at stake?

57. Where are mitigation costs factored in?

58. Tactics: eg, surprise, major contracts?

59. How can you counter negative efforts?

60. How are you predicting what future (work)loads will be?

61. Business and product development?

62. Who will be affected by the Chief Revenue Officer project?

63. Global influences?

64. What are the reimbursement requirements?

65. How much do resources cost?

66. Vital contracts and partners?

67. What is social & public accountability ?

68. Market developments?

69. Which resources are required?

70. How to measure the achievement of the Immediate Objective?

71. What do your organizations stakeholders do better than anyone else?

72. Financial reserves, likely returns?

2.0 Planning Process Group: Chief Revenue Officer

73. To what extent do the intervention objectives and strategies of the Chief Revenue Officer project respond to your organizations plans?

74. In which Chief Revenue Officer project management process group is the detailed Chief Revenue Officer project budget created?

75. What is the difference between the early schedule and late schedule?

76. Does it make any difference if you are successful?

77. How well defined and documented are the Chief Revenue Officer project management processes you chose to use?

78. What factors are contributing to progress or delay in the achievement of products and results?

79. To what extent has a PMO contributed to raising the quality of the design of the Chief Revenue Officer project?

80. What type of estimation method are you using?

81. Explanation: is what the Chief Revenue Officer project intents to solve a hard question?

82. If task x starts two days late, what is the effect on

the Chief Revenue Officer project end date?

83. Why do it Chief Revenue Officer projects fail?

84. Is the Chief Revenue Officer project supported by national and/or local organizations?

85. Is the duration of the program sufficient to ensure a cycle that will Chief Revenue Officer project the sustainability of the interventions?

86. Does the program have follow-up mechanisms (to verify the quality of the products, punctuality of delivery, etc.) to measure progress in the achievement of the envisaged results?

87. How do you integrate Chief Revenue Officer project Planning with the Iterative/Evolutionary SDLC?

88. If you are late, will anybody notice?

89. What will you do?

90. Contingency planning. if a risk event occurs, what will you do?

91. Are the follow-up indicators relevant and do they meet the quality needed to measure the outputs and outcomes of the Chief Revenue Officer project?

92. To what extent are the participating departments coordinating with each other?

2.1 Project Management Plan: Chief Revenue Officer

93. Why do you manage integration?

94. Are there any scope changes proposed for a previously authorized Chief Revenue Officer project?

95. Is there an incremental analysis/cost effectiveness analysis of proposed mitigation features based on an approved method and using an accepted model?

96. Will you add a schedule and diagram?

97. Does the implementation plan have an appropriate division of responsibilities?

98. Do the proposed changes from the Chief Revenue Officer project include any significant risks to safety?

99. How do you organize the costs in the Chief Revenue Officer project management plan?

100. Are there any windfall benefits that would accrue to the Chief Revenue Officer project sponsor or other parties?

101. What goes into your Chief Revenue Officer project Charter?

102. When is the Chief Revenue Officer project management plan created?

103. How well are you able to manage your risk?

104. Are there non-structural buyout or relocation recommendations?

105. Are the proposed Chief Revenue Officer project purposes different than a previously authorized Chief Revenue Officer project?

106. Is the engineering content at a feasibility level-of-detail, and is it sufficiently complete, to provide an adequate basis for the baseline cost estimate?

107. What data/reports/tools/etc. do program managers need?

108. Why Change?

109. Are comparable cost estimates used for comparing, screening and selecting alternative plans, and has a reasonable cost estimate been developed for the recommended plan?

110. What is Chief Revenue Officer project scope management?

111. Are cost risk analysis methods applied to develop contingencies for the estimated total Chief Revenue Officer project costs?

2.2 Scope Management Plan: Chief Revenue Officer

112. Have the scope, objectives, costs, benefits and impacts been communicated to all involved and/or impacted stakeholders and work groups?

113. Are risk triggers captured?

114. Are software metrics formally captured, analyzed and used as a basis for other Chief Revenue Officer project estimates?

115. Are corrective actions taken when actual results are substantially different from detailed Chief Revenue Officer project plan (variances)?

116. Is there a formal set of procedures supporting Issues Management?

117. Have the procedures for identifying budget variances been followed?

118. Has a provision been made to reassess Chief Revenue Officer project risks at various Chief Revenue Officer project stages?

119. Are the quality tools and methods identified in the Quality Plan appropriate to the Chief Revenue Officer project?

120. What weaknesses do you have?

121. Is there a Steering Committee in place?

122. Has process improvement efforts been completed before requirements efforts begin?

123. Is stakeholder involvement adequate?

124. Are tasks tracked by hours?

125. Describe the process for accepting the Chief Revenue Officer project deliverables. Will the Chief Revenue Officer project deliverables become accepted in writing?

126. Have the procedures for identifying variances from estimates & adjusting the detailed work program been followed?

127. Does a documented Chief Revenue Officer project organizational policy & plan (i.e. governance model) exist?

128. Is there any form of automated support for Issues Management?

129. Have all team members been part of identifying risks?

130. How many changes are you making?

2.3 Requirements Management Plan: Chief Revenue Officer

131. Are all the stakeholders ready for the transition into the user community?

132. What are you trying to do?

133. Do you have an agreed upon process for alerting the Chief Revenue Officer project Manager if a request for change in requirements leads to a product scope change?

134. Will the contractors involved take full responsibility?

135. Is the user satisfied?

136. When and how will a requirements baseline be established in this Chief Revenue Officer project?

137. Does the Chief Revenue Officer project have a Change Control process?

138. How knowledgeable is the primary Stakeholder(s) in the proposed application area?

139. Who will do the reporting and to whom will reports be delivered?

140. Is stakeholder risk tolerance an important factor for the requirements process in this Chief Revenue Officer project?

141. Subject to change control?

142. How will unresolved questions be handled once approval has been obtained?

143. How knowledgeable is the team in the proposed application area?

144. Will you use an assessment of the Chief Revenue Officer project environment as a tool to discover risk to the requirements process?

145. Business analysis scope?

146. Is infrastructure setup part of your Chief Revenue Officer project?

147. Are actual resource expenditures versus planned still acceptable?

148. Why manage requirements?

149. Who will initially review the Chief Revenue Officer project work or products to ensure it meets the applicable acceptance criteria?

150. What went wrong?

2.4 Requirements Documentation: Chief Revenue Officer

151. Is the requirement properly understood?

152. How do you get the user to tell you what they want?

153. If applicable; are there issues linked with the fact that this is an offshore Chief Revenue Officer project?

154. What facilities must be supported by the system?

155. What can tools do for us?

156. How will requirements be documented and who signs off on them?

157. Who is interacting with the system?

158. What are current process problems?

159. Has requirements gathering uncovered information that would necessitate changes?

160. Can you check system requirements?

161. What are the attributes of a customer?

162. What is effective documentation?

163. How can you document system requirements?

164. Who is involved?

165. Are there any requirements conflicts?

166. How much testing do you need to do to prove that your system is safe?

167. Is new technology needed?

168. Where do system and software requirements come from, what are sources?

169. What happens when requirements are wrong?

170. Are there legal issues?

2.5 Requirements Traceability Matrix: Chief Revenue Officer

171. How small is small enough?

172. How will it affect the stakeholders personally in career?

173. Why do you manage scope?

174. Describe the process for approving requirements so they can be added to the traceability matrix and Chief Revenue Officer project work can be performed. Will the Chief Revenue Officer project requirements become approved in writing?

175. How do you manage scope?

176. Is there a requirements traceability process in place?

177. What are the chronologies, contingencies, consequences, criteria?

178. Why use a WBS?

179. What is the WBS?

180. Do you have a clear understanding of all subcontracts in place?

181. What percentage of Chief Revenue Officer projects are producing traceability matrices between

requirements and other work products?

182. Will you use a Requirements Traceability Matrix?

2.6 Project Scope Statement: Chief Revenue Officer

183. Will you need a statement of work?

184. Will all Chief Revenue Officer project issues be unconditionally tracked through the issue resolution process?

185. Has the Chief Revenue Officer project scope statement been reviewed as part of the baseline process?

186. Have you been able to thoroughly document the Chief Revenue Officer projects assumptions and constraints?

187. Elements of scope management that deal with concept development ?

188. Has the format for tracking and monitoring schedules and costs been defined?

189. Elements that deal with providing the detail?

190. Is there an information system for the Chief Revenue Officer project?

191. Did your Chief Revenue Officer project ask for this?

192. What is the product of this Chief Revenue Officer project?

193. How often do you estimate that the scope might change, and why?

194. What should you drop in order to add something new?

195. Is the plan for Chief Revenue Officer project resources adequate?

196. Is the plan for your organization of the Chief Revenue Officer project resources adequate?

197. Will tasks be marked complete only after QA has been successfully completed?

198. Were key Chief Revenue Officer project stakeholders brought into the Chief Revenue Officer project Plan?

199. Will the risk status be reported to management on a regular and frequent basis?

200. Any new risks introduced or old risks impacted. Are there issues that could affect the existing requirements for the result, service, or product if the scope changes?

2.7 Assumption and Constraint Log: Chief Revenue Officer

201. What to do at recovery?

202. Are there standards for code development?

203. How do you design an auditing system?

204. What does an audit system look like?

205. Is this model reasonable?

206. What strengths do you have?

207. How can you prevent/fix violations?

208. What do you audit?

209. Are there cosmetic errors that hinder readability and comprehension?

210. Are there nonconformance issues?

211. Have all stakeholders been identified?

212. Contradictory information between document sections?

213. Have all involved stakeholders and work groups committed to the Chief Revenue Officer project?

214. Does the traceability documentation describe

the tool and/or mechanism to be used to capture traceability throughout the life cycle?

215. Does the Chief Revenue Officer project have a formal Chief Revenue Officer project Plan?

216. Is the process working, and people are not executing in compliance of the process?

217. Can you perform this task or activity in a more effective manner?

218. Have Chief Revenue Officer project management standards and procedures been established and documented?

219. After observing execution of process, is it in compliance with the documented Plan?

2.8 Work Breakdown Structure: Chief Revenue Officer

220. What has to be done?

221. When do you stop?

222. How far down?

223. How big is a work-package?

224. Is the work breakdown structure (wbs) defined and is the scope of the Chief Revenue Officer project clear with assigned deliverable owners?

225. What is the probability of completing the Chief Revenue Officer project in less that xx days?

226. How will you and your Chief Revenue Officer project team define the Chief Revenue Officer projects scope and work breakdown structure?

227. Do you need another level?

228. Who has to do it?

229. Can you make it?

230. Is it a change in scope?

231. How much detail?

232. What is the probability that the Chief Revenue

Officer project duration will exceed xx weeks?

233. Where does it take place?

234. When does it have to be done?

235. When would you develop a Work Breakdown Structure?

236. Why is it useful?

237. Why would you develop a Work Breakdown Structure?

2.9 WBS Dictionary: Chief Revenue Officer

238. Are records maintained to show how management reserves are used?

239. What went right?

240. Does the contractor have procedures which permit identification of recurring or non-recurring costs as necessary?

241. Are current budgets resulting from changes to the authorized work and/or internal replanning, reconcilable to original budgets for specified reporting items?

242. Are overhead costs budgets established on a basis consistent with anticipated direct business base?

243. Does the accounting system provide a basis for auditing records of direct costs chargeable to the contract?

244. Are current work performance indicators and goals relatable to original goals as modified by contractual changes, replanning, and reprogramming actions?

245. Where engineering standards or other internal work measurement systems are used, is there a formal relationship between corresponding values and work

package budgets?

246. Is future work which cannot be planned in detail subdivided to the extent practicable for budgeting and scheduling purposes?

247. Should you have a test for each code module?

248. What is the goal?

249. Are data elements summarized through the functional organizational structure for progressively higher levels of management?

250. Wbs elements contractually specified for reporting of status to you (lowest level only)?

251. Is each control account assigned to a single organizational element directly responsible for the work and identifiable to a single element of the CWBS?

252. Does the scheduling system provide for the identification of work progress against technical and other milestones, and also provide for forecasts of completion dates of scheduled work?

253. Budgeted cost for work performed?

254. Do procedures specify under what circumstances replanning of open work packages may occur, and the methods to be followed?

255. Are the wbs and organizational levels for application of the Chief Revenue Officer projected overhead costs identified?

256. The already stated responsible for overhead performance control of related costs?

2.10 Schedule Management Plan: Chief Revenue Officer

257. Have activity relationships and interdependencies within tasks been adequately identified?

258. Is the plan consistent with industry best practices?

259. Are software metrics formally captured, analyzed and used as a basis for other Chief Revenue Officer project estimates?

260. Is the quality assurance team identified?

261. Have Chief Revenue Officer project management standards and procedures been identified / established and documented?

262. Have all necessary approvals been obtained?

263. Are the Chief Revenue Officer project team members located locally to the users/stakeholders?

264. Are all payments made according to the contract(s)?

265. Does the Chief Revenue Officer project have a Quality Culture?

266. Where is the scheduling tool and who has access to it to view it?

267. Are estimating assumptions and constraints captured?

268. What is the difference between % Complete and % work?

269. Are vendor contract reports, reviews and visits conducted periodically?

270. Is a process for scheduling and reporting defined, including forms and formats?

271. Are issues raised, assessed, actioned, and resolved in a timely and efficient manner?

272. Does the business case include how the Chief Revenue Officer project aligns with your organizations strategic goals & objectives?

273. Is there an approved case?

274. What threats might prevent you from getting there?

275. What happens if a warning is triggered?

2.11 Activity List: Chief Revenue Officer

276. When do the individual activities need to start and finish?

277. In what sequence?

278. Can you determine the activity that must finish, before this activity can start?

279. What are you counting on?

280. What is the probability the Chief Revenue Officer project can be completed in xx weeks?

281. Are the required resources available or need to be acquired?

282. Where will it be performed?

283. When will the work be performed?

284. How will it be performed?

285. How detailed should a Chief Revenue Officer project get?

286. The wbs is developed as part of a joint planning session. and how do you know that youhave done this right?

287. What did not go as well?

288. How can the Chief Revenue Officer project be displayed graphically to better visualize the activities?

289. Who will perform the work?

290. What are the critical bottleneck activities?

291. What went well?

292. How much slack is available in the Chief Revenue Officer project?

293. How should ongoing costs be monitored to try to keep the Chief Revenue Officer project within budget?

294. How do you determine the late start (LS) for each activity?

2.12 Activity Attributes: Chief Revenue Officer

295. What is missing?

296. Resource is assigned to?

297. What is your organizations history in doing similar activities?

298. What is the general pattern here?

299. What conclusions/generalizations can you draw from this?

300. Can you re-assign any activities to another resource to resolve an over-allocation?

301. Why?

302. Do you feel very comfortable with your prediction?

303. Are the required resources available?

304. Activity: what is Missing?

305. Activity: what is In the Bag?

306. Activity: fair or not fair?

307. Can more resources be added?

308. Have constraints been applied to the start and finish milestones for the phases?

309. Time for overtime?

310. How difficult will it be to complete specific activities on this Chief Revenue Officer project?

311. How else could the items be grouped?

312. Does your organization of the data change its meaning?

2.13 Milestone List: Chief Revenue Officer

313. Milestone pages should display the UserID of the person who added the milestone. Does a report or query exist that provides this audit information?

314. How soon can the activity finish?

315. Continuity, supply chain robustness?

316. Political effects?

317. Calculate how long can activity be delayed?

318. It is to be a narrative text providing the crucial aspects of your Chief Revenue Officer project proposal answering what, who, how, when and where?

319. How late can the activity start?

320. Loss of key staff?

321. Competitive advantages?

322. What would happen if a delivery of material was one week late?

323. Describe the industry you are in and the market growth opportunities. What is the market for your technology, product or service?

324. How will you get the word out to customers?

325. How do you manage time?

326. Can you derive how soon can the whole Chief Revenue Officer project finish?

327. Insurmountable weaknesses?

328. What has been done so far?

329. Do you foresee any technical risks or developmental challenges?

2.14 Network Diagram: Chief Revenue Officer

330. What can be done concurrently?

331. What are the Key Success Factors?

332. What job or jobs follow it?

333. How difficult will it be to do specific activities on this Chief Revenue Officer project?

334. What activities must occur simultaneously with this activity?

335. What activities must follow this activity?

336. Will crashing x weeks return more in benefits than it costs?

337. Review the logical flow of the network diagram. Take a look at which activities you have first and then sequence the activities. Do they make sense?

338. What is the completion time?

339. How confident can you be in your milestone dates and the delivery date?

340. What controls the start and finish of a job?

341. Exercise: what is the probability that the Chief Revenue Officer project duration will exceed xx

weeks?

342. Planning: who, how long, what to do?

343. Are the gantt chart and/or network diagram updated periodically and used to assess the overall Chief Revenue Officer project timetable?

344. Which type of network diagram allows you to depict four types of dependencies?

345. Where do schedules come from?

346. Can you calculate the confidence level?

347. What job or jobs could run concurrently?

2.15 Activity Resource Requirements: Chief Revenue Officer

348. When does monitoring begin?

349. How do you handle petty cash?

350. Organizational Applicability?

351. How many signatures do you require on a check and does this match what is in your policy and procedures?

352. What are constraints that you might find during the Human Resource Planning process?

353. Why do you do that?

354. Anything else?

355. Are there unresolved issues that need to be addressed?

356. Other support in specific areas?

357. What is the Work Plan Standard?

358. Do you use tools like decomposition and rolling-wave planning to produce the activity list and other outputs?

359. Is there anything planned that does not need to be here?

360. Which logical relationship does the PDM use most often?

2.16 Resource Breakdown Structure: Chief Revenue Officer

361. Any changes from stakeholders?

362. What is the purpose of assigning and documenting responsibility?

363. Which resources should be in the resource pool?

364. What is the number one predictor of a groups productivity?

365. Who needs what information?

366. What defines a successful Chief Revenue Officer project?

367. Who delivers the information?

368. What can you do to improve productivity?

369. Who is allowed to see what data about which resources?

370. Why time management?

371. What is each stakeholders desired outcome for the Chief Revenue Officer project?

372. The list could probably go on, but, the thing that you would most like to know is, How long & How much?

373. Why do you do it?

374. Who will use the system?

375. What defines a successful Chief Revenue Officer project?

376. Which resource planning tool provides information on resource responsibility and accountability?

377. How can this help you with team building?

2.17 Activity Duration Estimates: Chief Revenue Officer

378. What should be done NEXT?

379. Would you rate yourself as being risk-averse, risk-neutral, or risk-seeking?

380. What is the duration of the critical path for this Chief Revenue Officer project?

381. Do checklists exist that list frequently performed activities?

382. If you plan to take the PMP exam soon, what should you do to prepare?

383. Which is correct?

384. Are procedures documented for managing risks?

385. Are activity duration estimates documented?

386. Why is it important to determine activity sequencing on Chief Revenue Officer projects?

387. Who will provide training for the new application?

388. Briefly describe some key events in the history of Chief Revenue Officer project management. What Chief Revenue Officer project was the first to use modern Chief Revenue Officer project management?

389. Are procedures defined by which the Chief Revenue Officer project scope may be changed?

390. Who will be the main sponsor for it?

391. Are training needs identified when resources do not have the required skills to complete Chief Revenue Officer project activities?

392. How does a Chief Revenue Officer project life cycle differ from a product life cycle?

393. Are tools and techniques defined for gathering, integrating and distributing Chief Revenue Officer project outputs?

394. What tasks can take place concurrently?

395. What is pmp certification, and why do you think the number of people earning it has grown so much in the past ten years?

396. Why do you think schedule issues often cause the most conflicts on Chief Revenue Officer projects?

397. What are the main types of contracts if you do decide to outsource?

2.18 Duration Estimating Worksheet: Chief Revenue Officer

398. What info is needed?

399. Why estimate costs?

400. Is a construction detail attached (to aid in explanation)?

401. What is next?

402. Define the work as completely as possible. What work will be included in the Chief Revenue Officer project?

403. Why estimate time and cost?

404. Is this operation cost effective?

405. Does the Chief Revenue Officer project provide innovative ways for stakeholders to overcome obstacles or deliver better outcomes?

406. What utility impacts are there?

407. What is your role?

408. What is the total time required to complete the Chief Revenue Officer project if no delays occur?

409. Is the Chief Revenue Officer project responsive to community need?

410. How should ongoing costs be monitored to try to keep the Chief Revenue Officer project within budget?

411. When does your organization expect to be able to complete it?

412. Do any colleagues have experience with your organization and/or RFPs?

413. Done before proceeding with this activity or what can be done concurrently?

414. Value pocket identification & quantification what are value pockets?

2.19 Project Schedule: Chief Revenue Officer

415. Chief Revenue Officer project work estimates Who is managing the work estimate quality of work tasks in the Chief Revenue Officer project schedule?

416. Are activities connected because logic dictates the order in which others occur?

417. How can you address that situation?

418. Why do you think schedule issues often cause the most conflicts on Chief Revenue Officer projects?

419. Are all remaining durations correct?

420. To what degree is do you feel the entire team was committed to the Chief Revenue Officer project schedule?

421. Month Chief Revenue Officer project take?

422. How do you know that youhave done this right?

423. How can you fix it?

424. Did the final product meet or exceed user expectations?

425. How much slack is available in the Chief Revenue Officer project?

426. Meet requirements?

427. Change management required?

428. How does a Chief Revenue Officer project get to be a year late ?

429. What is risk?

430. Schedule/cost recovery?

431. Are you working on the right risks?

432. Eliminate unnecessary activities. Are there activities that came from a template or previous Chief Revenue Officer project that are not applicable on this phase of this Chief Revenue Officer project?

2.20 Cost Management Plan: Chief Revenue Officer

433. Are risk oriented checklists used during risk identification?

434. Were Chief Revenue Officer project team members involved in the development of activity & task decomposition?

435. Are metrics used to evaluate and manage Vendors?

436. Are schedule deliverables actually delivered?

437. Is it a Chief Revenue Officer project?

438. Was the Chief Revenue Officer project schedule reviewed by all stakeholders and formally accepted?

439. Risk rating?

440. Is a pmo (Chief Revenue Officer project management office) in place and provide oversight to the Chief Revenue Officer project?

441. Has a structured approach been used to break work effort into manageable components (WBS)?

442. Vac -variance at completion, how much over/ under budget do you expect to be?

443. Contracting method – what contracting method

is to be used for the contracts?

444. Was your organizations estimating methodology being used and followed?

445. Are the appropriate IT resources adequate to meet planned commitments?

446. Are all key components of a Quality Assurance Plan present?

447. Have the key functions and capabilities been defined and assigned to each release or iteration?

448. Is a stakeholder management plan in place that covers topics?

449. Is your organization certified as a supplier, wholesaler, regular dealer, or manufacturer of corresponding products/supplies?

2.21 Activity Cost Estimates: Chief Revenue Officer

450. If you are asked to lower your estimate because the price is too high, what are your options?

451. Did the consultant work with local staff to develop local capacity?

452. Are cost subtotals needed?

453. What were things that you need to improve?

454. Will you need to provide essential services information about activities?

455. What happens if you cannot produce the documentation for the single audit?

456. Specific - is the objective clear in terms of what, how, when, and where the situation will be changed?

457. Why do you manage cost?

458. What is the activity inventory?

459. Would you hire them again?

460. Were the tasks or work products prepared by the consultant useful?

461. Where can you get activity reports?

462. Who determines the quality and expertise of contractors?

463. What makes a good expected result statement?

464. The impact and what actions were taken?

465. Will you use any tools, such as Chief Revenue Officer project management software, to assist in capturing Earned Value metrics?

466. How do you allocate indirect costs to activities?

467. Scope statement only direct or indirect costs as well?

2.22 Cost Estimating Worksheet: Chief Revenue Officer

468. What can be included?

469. Can a trend be established from historical performance data on the selected measure and are the criteria for using trend analysis or forecasting methods met?

470. What is the estimated labor cost today based upon this information?

471. What will others want?

472. Who is best positioned to know and assist in identifying corresponding factors?

473. Is the Chief Revenue Officer project responsive to community need?

474. What is the purpose of estimating?

475. Does the Chief Revenue Officer project provide innovative ways for stakeholders to overcome obstacles or deliver better outcomes?

476. What costs are to be estimated?

477. Is it feasible to establish a control group arrangement?

478. What happens to any remaining funds not used?

479. Will the Chief Revenue Officer project collaborate with the local community and leverage resources?

480. Identify the timeframe necessary to monitor progress and collect data to determine how the selected measure has changed?

481. What additional Chief Revenue Officer project(s) could be initiated as a result of this Chief Revenue Officer project?

482. Ask: are others positioned to know, are others credible, and will others cooperate?

483. How will the results be shared and to whom?

2.23 Cost Baseline: Chief Revenue Officer

484. Does a process exist for establishing a cost baseline to measure Chief Revenue Officer project performance?

485. Are you meeting with your team regularly?

486. Should a more thorough impact analysis be conducted?

487. Review your risk triggers -have your risks changed?

488. Has the Chief Revenue Officer project (or Chief Revenue Officer project phase) been evaluated against each objective established in the product description and Integrated Chief Revenue Officer project Plan?

489. Pcs for your new business. what would the life cycle costs be?

490. Have the lessons learned been filed with the Chief Revenue Officer project Management Office?

491. Escalation criteria met?

492. Is the requested change request a result of changes in other Chief Revenue Officer project(s)?

493. What is it ?

494. How long are you willing to wait before you find out were late?

495. Does the suggested change request seem to represent a necessary enhancement to the product?

496. How likely is it to go wrong?

497. What do you want to measure ?

498. Has the actual cost of the Chief Revenue Officer project (or Chief Revenue Officer project phase) been tallied and compared to the approved budget?

499. Chief Revenue Officer project goals -should others be reconsidered?

500. When should cost estimates be developed?

501. Does it impact schedule, cost, quality?

2.24 Quality Management Plan: Chief Revenue Officer

502. Does the plan conform to standards?

503. Modifications to the requirements?

504. What are your organizations current levels and trends for the already stated measures related to employee wellbeing, satisfaction, and development?

505. What key performance indicators does your organization use to measure, manage, and improve key processes?

506. What data do you gather/use/compile?

507. Does the program use modeling in the permitting or decision-making processes?

508. Does a documented Chief Revenue Officer project organizational policy & plan (i.e. governance model) exist?

509. How do you ensure that your sampling methods and procedures meet your data needs?

510. What worked well?

511. How is equipment calibrated?

512. How are senior leaders, employees, and your organization involved in supporting the community?

513. No superfluous information or marketing narrative?

514. Written by multiple authors and in multiple writing styles?

515. What is positive about the current process?

516. How does your organization make it easy for customers to seek assistance or complain?

517. Is staff trained on the software technologies that are being used on the Chief Revenue Officer project?

518. Who gets results of work?

519. Were there any deficiencies / issues in prior years self-assessment?

520. Does the Chief Revenue Officer project have a formal Chief Revenue Officer project Plan?

521. How are training records kept?

2.25 Quality Metrics: Chief Revenue Officer

522. Has it met internal or external standards?

523. How do you measure?

524. Are there any open risk issues?

525. Are there already quality metrics available that detect nonlinear embeddings and trends similar to the users perception?

526. Did the team meet the Chief Revenue Officer project success criteria documented in the Quality Metrics Matrix?

527. Who notifies stakeholders of normal and abnormal results?

528. What metrics do you measure?

529. How exactly do you define when differences exist?

530. How is it being measured?

531. Which are the right metrics to use?

532. When will the Final Guidance will be issued?

533. How effective are your security tests?

534. There are many reasons to shore up quality-related metrics, and what metrics are important?

535. Is quality culture a competitive advantage?

536. What approved evidence based screening tools can be used?

537. Which data do others need in one place to target areas of improvement?

538. The metrics–what is being considered?

539. Where did complaints, returns and warranty claims come from?

540. Are quality metrics defined?

541. Have alternatives been defined in the event that failure occurs?

2.26 Process Improvement Plan: Chief Revenue Officer

542. What personnel are the sponsors for that initiative?

543. Has a process guide to collect the data been developed?

544. What personnel are the champions for the initiative?

545. What is the return on investment?

546. Does your process ensure quality?

547. Are there forms and procedures to collect and record the data?

548. The motive is determined by asking, Why do you want to achieve this goal?

549. If a process improvement framework is being used, which elements will help the problems and goals listed?

550. Does explicit definition of the measures exist?

551. Has the time line required to move measurement results from the points of collection to databases or users been established?

552. Are you making progress on the goals?

553. What is quality and how will you ensure it?

554. How do you manage quality?

555. What makes people good SPI coaches?

556. Purpose of goal: the motive is determined by asking, why do you want to achieve this goal?

557. Modeling current processes is great, and will you ever see a return on that investment?

558. Are you making progress on the improvement framework?

559. What lessons have you learned so far?

2.27 Responsibility Assignment Matrix: Chief Revenue Officer

560. Detailed schedules which support control account and work package start and completion dates/events?

561. Chief Revenue Officer projected economic escalation?

562. What tool can show you individual and group allocations?

563. Are all authorized tasks assigned to identified organizational elements?

564. Wbs elements contractually specified for reporting of status (lowest level only)?

565. Does a missing responsibility indicate that the current Chief Revenue Officer project is not yet fully understood?

566. Are there any drawbacks to using a responsibility assignment matrix?

567. Are the requirements for all items of overhead established by rational, traceable processes?

568. Too many as: does a proper segregation of duties exist?

569. Most people let you know when others re too

busy, and are others really too busy?

570. Incurrence of actual indirect costs in excess of budgets, by element of expense?

571. Do all the identified groups or people really need to be consulted?

572. Authorization to proceed with all authorized work?

573. Is the entire contract planned in time-phased control accounts to the extent practicable?

574. Identify potential or actual budget-based and time-based schedule variances?

575. Changes in the direct base to which overhead costs are allocated?

576. Are people afraid to let you know when others are under allocated?

577. Too many is: do all the identified roles need to be routinely informed or only in exceptional circumstances?

578. If a role has only Signing-off, or only Communicating responsibility and has no Performing, Accountable, or Monitoring responsibility, is it necessary?

579. Major functional areas of contract effort?

2.28 Roles and Responsibilities: Chief Revenue Officer

580. What should you do now to prepare for your career 5+ years from now?

581. Implementation of actions: Who are the responsible units?

582. Is the data complete?

583. Once the responsibilities are defined for the Chief Revenue Officer project, have the deliverables, roles and responsibilities been clearly communicated to every participant?

584. Are Chief Revenue Officer project team roles and responsibilities identified and documented?

585. What specific behaviors did you observe?

586. Be specific; avoid generalities. Thank you and great work alone are insufficient. What exactly do you appreciate and why?

587. How is your work-life balance?

588. Have you ever been a part of this team?

589. To decide whether to use a quality measurement, ask how will you know when it is achieved?

590. Who: who is involved?

591. Are your budgets supportive of a culture of quality data?

592. Concern: where are you limited or have no authority, where you can not influence?

593. Is there a training program in place for stakeholders covering expectations, roles and responsibilities and any addition knowledge others need to be good stakeholders?

594. What is working well within your organizations performance management system?

595. Are governance roles and responsibilities documented?

596. Authority: what areas/Chief Revenue Officer projects in your work do you have the authority to decide upon and act on the already stated decisions?

597. Was the expectation clearly communicated?

598. What expectations were NOT met?

2.29 Human Resource Management Plan: Chief Revenue Officer

599. What is the boss?

600. Is the communication plan being followed?

601. Has a quality assurance plan been developed for the Chief Revenue Officer project?

602. Do Chief Revenue Officer project teams & team members report on status / activities / progress?

603. Has the schedule been baselined?

604. Chief Revenue Officer project Objectives?

605. Are people being developed to meet the challenges of the future?

606. Are people motivated to meet the current and future challenges?

607. Were stakeholders aware and supportive of the principles and practices of modern cost estimation?

608. Identify who is needed on the core Chief Revenue Officer project team to complete Chief Revenue Officer project deliverables and achieve its goals and objectives. What skills, knowledge and experiences are required?

609. Is a payment system in place with proper reviews

and approvals?

610. Quality assurance overheads?

611. Are the payment terms being followed?

612. Are the schedule estimates reasonable given the Chief Revenue Officer project?

613. Is pert / critical path or equivalent methodology being used?

2.30 Communications Management Plan: Chief Revenue Officer

614. What to learn?

615. Why do you manage communications?

616. What is Chief Revenue Officer project communications management?

617. Which team member will work with each stakeholder?

618. Are there too many who have an interest in some aspect of your work?

619. Which stakeholders are thought leaders, influences, or early adopters?

620. Are others part of the communications management plan?

621. Who needs to know and how much?

622. Do you feel more overwhelmed by stakeholders?

623. Who did you turn to if you had questions?

624. Can you think of other people who might have concerns or interests?

625. Do you then often overlook a key stakeholder or stakeholder group?

626. Why is stakeholder engagement important?

627. Where do team members get information?

628. Are there potential barriers between the team and the stakeholder?

629. Do you have members of your team responsible for certain stakeholders?

630. In your work, how much time is spent on stakeholder identification?

631. Are stakeholders internal or external?

632. What communications method?

633. Who have you worked with in past, similar initiatives?

2.31 Risk Management Plan: Chief Revenue Officer

634. Prioritized components/features?

635. How can the process be made more effective or less cumbersome (process improvements)?

636. Costs associated with late delivery or a defective product?

637. Are testing tools available and suitable?

638. Is the necessary data being captured and is it complete and accurate?

639. Do the people have the right combinations of skills?

640. How is the audit profession changing?

641. What is the likelihood?

642. How is risk identification performed?

643. Are tool mentors available?

644. Are Chief Revenue Officer project requirements stable?

645. User involvement: do you have the right users?

646. What will drive change?

647. Is security a central objective?

648. Are the reports useful and easy to read?

649. Do you train all developers in the process?

650. If you can not fix it, how do you do it differently?

651. Are some people working on multiple Chief Revenue Officer projects?

652. Are tools for analysis and design available?

653. Litigation – what is the probability that lawsuits will cause problems or delays in the Chief Revenue Officer project?

2.32 Risk Register: Chief Revenue Officer

654. Budget and schedule: what are the estimated costs and schedules for performing risk-related activities?

655. What are the major risks facing the Chief Revenue Officer project?

656. Schedule impact/severity estimated range (workdays) assume the event happens, what is the potential impact?

657. Who is going to do it?

658. What may happen or not go according to plan?

659. Assume the risk event or situation happens, what would the impact be?

660. Are there any gaps in the evidence?

661. Do you require further engagement?

662. Who needs to know about this?

663. Market risk -will the new service or product be useful to your organization or marketable to others?

664. Risk probability and impact: how will the probabilities and impacts of risk items be assessed?

665. When would you develop a risk register?

666. Recovery actions - planned actions taken once a risk has occurred to allow you to move on. What should you do after?

667. Severity Prediction?

668. What further options might be available for responding to the risk?

669. Technology risk -is the Chief Revenue Officer project technically feasible?

670. What are your key risks/show istoppers and what is being done to manage them?

671. What is the probability and impact of the risk occurring?

672. Are there any knock-on effects/impact on any of the other areas?

2.33 Probability and Impact Assessment: Chief Revenue Officer

673. What things might go wrong?

674. How would you suggest monitoring for risk transition indicators?

675. Why has this particular mode of contracting been chosen?

676. What are your data sources?

677. Is the customer willing to commit significant time to the requirements gathering process?

678. What are the preparations required for facing difficulties?

679. How are you working with risks?

680. What will be the impact or consequence if the risk occurs?

681. How do risks change during a Chief Revenue Officer project life cycle?

682. What is the experience (performance, attitude, business ethics, etc.) in the past with contractors?

683. What should be the requirement of organizational restructuring as each subChief Revenue Officer project goes through a different

lifecycle phase?

684. Do you have a consistent repeatable process that is actually used?

685. Is the customer willing to establish rapid communication links with the developer?

686. How much risk do others need to take?

687. How is the Chief Revenue Officer project going to be managed?

688. Sensitivity analysis -which risks will have the most impact on the Chief Revenue Officer project?

689. Monitoring of the overall Chief Revenue Officer project status – are there any changes in the Chief Revenue Officer project that can effect and cause new possible risks?

690. Are the risk data timely and relevant?

691. Can this technology be absorbed with current level of expertise available in your organization?

2.34 Probability and Impact Matrix: Chief Revenue Officer

692. What are the current demands of the customer?

693. Pay attention to the quality of the plans: is the content complete, or does it seem to be lacking detail?

694. What is the industrial relations prevailing in this organization?

695. Do you use any methods to analyze risks?

696. Can you avoid altogether some things that might go wrong?

697. What changes in the regulation are forthcoming?

698. Do you have specific methods that you use for each phase of the process?

699. The customer requests a change to the Chief Revenue Officer project that would increase the Chief Revenue Officer project risk. Which should you do before ass the others?

700. What risks were tracked?

701. How will economic events and trends likely affect the Chief Revenue Officer project?

702. Will there be an increase in the political

conservatism?

703. Are team members trained in the use of the tools?

704. What are the probable external agencies to act as Chief Revenue Officer project manager?

705. Is the number of people on the Chief Revenue Officer project team adequate to do the job?

706. Has the need for the Chief Revenue Officer project been properly established?

707. Are the risk data complete?

708. Which of the risk factors can be avoided altogether?

2.35 Risk Data Sheet: Chief Revenue Officer

709. What were the Causes that contributed?

710. What are you here for (Mission)?

711. How do you handle product safely?

712. What are your core values?

713. What is the chance that it will happen?

714. Has a sensitivity analysis been carried out?

715. What actions can be taken to eliminate or remove risk?

716. What will be the consequences if the risk happens?

717. What are you trying to achieve (Objectives)?

718. How reliable is the data source?

719. What can happen?

720. Has the most cost-effective solution been chosen?

721. What will be the consequences if it happens?

722. How can hazards be reduced?

723. What if client refuses?

724. Is the data sufficiently specified in terms of the type of failure being analyzed, and its frequency or probability?

725. Risk of what?

726. During work activities could hazards exist?

727. Do effective diagnostic tests exist?

728. What was measured?

2.36 Procurement Management Plan: Chief Revenue Officer

729. Are changes in deliverable commitments agreed to by all affected groups & individuals?

730. Does the schedule include Chief Revenue Officer project management time and change request analysis time?

731. Do Chief Revenue Officer project teams & team members report on status / activities / progress?

732. If independent estimates will be needed as evaluation criteria, who will prepare them and when?

733. What were things that you did very well and want to do the same again on the next Chief Revenue Officer project?

734. Have Chief Revenue Officer project team accountabilities & responsibilities been clearly defined?

735. Are stakeholders aware and supportive of the principles and practices of modern software estimation?

736. Are adequate resources provided for the quality assurance function?

737. Are software metrics formally captured, analyzed and used as a basis for other Chief Revenue Officer

project estimates?

738. Is there a procurement management plan in place?

739. Are procurement deliverables arriving on time and to specification?

740. Is an industry recognized mechanized support tool(s) being used for Chief Revenue Officer project scheduling & tracking?

741. Similar Chief Revenue Officer projects?

742. Public engagement – did you get it right?

743. Are the schedule estimates reasonable given the Chief Revenue Officer project?

744. Has Chief Revenue Officer project success criteria been defined?

2.37 Source Selection Criteria: Chief Revenue Officer

745. How should the oral presentations be handled?

746. Is the offeror pricing what is technically proposed?

747. How do you facilitate evaluation against published criteria?

748. Are resultant proposal revisions allowed?

749. Is there collaboration among your evaluators?

750. Do proposed hours support content and schedule?

751. Are there any specific considerations that precludes offers from being selected as the awardee?

752. What information is to be provided and when should it be provided?

753. Do you have designated specific forms or worksheets?

754. Are types/quantities of material, facilities appropriate?

755. How should oral presentations be evaluated?

756. What information may not be provided?

757. What is the role of counsel in the procurement process?

758. What are the most common types of rating systems?

759. How will you decide an evaluators write up is sufficient?

760. What should a Draft Request for Proposal (DRFP) include?

761. How much past performance information should be requested?

762. How do you ensure an integrated assessment of proposals?

763. What is the last item a Chief Revenue Officer project manager must do to finalize Chief Revenue Officer project close-out?

764. What are the most critical evaluation criteria that prove to be tiebreakers in the evaluation of proposals?

2.38 Stakeholder Management Plan: Chief Revenue Officer

765. Detail warranty and/or maintenance periods?

766. Are mitigation strategies identified?

767. Is there a formal set of procedures supporting Stakeholder Management?

768. Are non-critical path items updated and agreed upon with the teams?

769. Are there checklists created to demine if all quality processes are followed?

770. Is an industry recognized mechanized support tool(s) being used for Chief Revenue Officer project scheduling & tracking?

771. Does the Chief Revenue Officer project have a Quality Culture?

772. Why would you develop a Chief Revenue Officer project Execution Plan?

773. Were the budget estimates reasonable?

774. How will you engage this stakeholder and gain commitment?

775. Are decisions captured in a decisions log?

776. Do Chief Revenue Officer project managers participating in the Chief Revenue Officer project know the Chief Revenue Officer projects true status first hand?

777. Does the system design reflect the requirements?

778. Does the Chief Revenue Officer project have a formal Chief Revenue Officer project Charter?

2.39 Change Management Plan: Chief Revenue Officer

779. Who might present the most resistance?

780. Change invariability confront many relationships especially the already stated that require a set of behaviours What roles with in your organization are affected and how?

781. What does a resilient organization look like?

782. Has the training provider been established?

783. How far reaching in your organization is the change?

784. What prerequisite knowledge or training is required?

785. What will be the preferred method of delivery?

786. Are work location changes required?

787. What is the worst thing that can happen if you communicate information?

788. Who will fund the training?

789. Has a training need analysis been carried out?

790. Will all field readiness criteria have been practically met prior to training roll-out?

791. What prerequisite knowledge do corresponding groups need?

792. Do you need new systems?

793. Have the business unit contacts been selected and notified?

794. What can you do to minimise misinterpretation and negative perceptions?

795. Why is the initiative is being undertaken - What are the business drivers?

796. Where do you want to be?

797. Do you need a new organization structure?

3.0 Executing Process Group: Chief Revenue Officer

798. What are the main processes included in Chief Revenue Officer project quality management?

799. What are crucial elements of successful Chief Revenue Officer project plan execution?

800. Do the products created live up to the necessary quality?

801. Will new hardware or software be required for servers or client machines?

802. What Chief Revenue Officer projects and services are in the portfolio of your organization?

803. If action is called for, what form should it take?

804. Who are the Chief Revenue Officer project stakeholders?

805. What are the challenges Chief Revenue Officer project teams face?

806. Does software appear easy to learn?

807. Why should Chief Revenue Officer project managers strive to make jobs look easy?

808. How well did the team follow the chosen processes?

809. How well did the chosen processes produce the expected results?

810. Who will provide training?

811. What are the Chief Revenue Officer project management deliverables of each process group?

812. How do you measure difficulty?

813. Will a new application be developed using existing hardware, software, and networks?

814. Do the partners have sufficient financial capacity to keep up the benefits produced by the programme?

815. Does the case present a realistic scenario?

3.1 Team Member Status Report: Chief Revenue Officer

816. Does the product, good, or service already exist within your organization?

817. Does every department have to have a Chief Revenue Officer project Manager on staff?

818. How does this product, good, or service meet the needs of the Chief Revenue Officer project and your organization as a whole?

819. Does your organization have the means (staff, money, contract, etc.) to produce or to acquire the product, good, or service?

820. Are your organizations Chief Revenue Officer projects more successful over time?

821. Do you have an Enterprise Chief Revenue Officer project Management Office (EPMO)?

822. Is there evidence that staff is taking a more professional approach toward management of your organizations Chief Revenue Officer projects?

823. When a teams productivity and success depend on collaboration and the efficient flow of information, what generally fails them?

824. How much risk is involved?

825. How will resource planning be done?

826. Why is it to be done?

827. What is to be done?

828. Will the staff do training or is that done by a third party?

829. How it is to be done?

830. The problem with Reward & Recognition Programs is that the truly deserving people all too often get left out. How can you make it practical?

831. Are the products of your organizations Chief Revenue Officer projects meeting customers objectives?

832. How can you make it practical?

833. What specific interest groups do you have in place?

834. Are the attitudes of staff regarding Chief Revenue Officer project work improving?

3.2 Change Request: Chief Revenue Officer

835. Are there requirements attributes that can discriminate between high and low reliability?

836. What are the requirements for urgent changes?

837. Which requirements attributes affect the risk to reliability the most?

838. How is quality being addressed on the Chief Revenue Officer project?

839. What is the purpose of change control?

840. Are you implementing itil processes?

841. Why do you want to have a change control system?

842. Who needs to approve change requests?

843. How many times must the change be modified or presented to the change control board before it is approved?

844. How are changes requested (forms, method of communication)?

845. What is the relationship between requirements attributes and reliability?

846. Will there be a change request form in use?

847. How can changes be graded?

848. Are there requirements attributes that are strongly related to the complexity and size?

849. Who has responsibility for approving and ranking changes?

850. What is the change request log?

851. Are change requests logged and managed?

852. Why control change across the life cycle?

853. What are the basic mechanics of the Change Advisory Board (CAB)?

854. How fast will change requests be approved?

3.3 Change Log: Chief Revenue Officer

855. How does this relate to the standards developed for specific business processes?

856. Is the change request within Chief Revenue Officer project scope?

857. When was the request approved?

858. Is the requested change request a result of changes in other Chief Revenue Officer project(s)?

859. Where do changes come from?

860. Is the change backward compatible without limitations?

861. When was the request submitted?

862. Is the change request open, closed or pending?

863. Does the suggested change request represent a desired enhancement to the products functionality?

864. Is the submitted change a new change or a modification of a previously approved change?

865. How does this change affect scope?

866. Who initiated the change request?

867. Do the described changes impact on the integrity or security of the system?

868. How does this change affect the timeline of the schedule?

869. Will the Chief Revenue Officer project fail if the change request is not executed?

870. Is this a mandatory replacement?

3.4 Decision Log: Chief Revenue Officer

871. What is the average size of your matters in an applicable measurement?

872. What is your overall strategy for quality control / quality assurance procedures?

873. Meeting purpose; why does this team meet?

874. Which variables make a critical difference?

875. At what point in time does loss become unacceptable?

876. How does an increasing emphasis on cost containment influence the strategies and tactics used?

877. Is everything working as expected?

878. How do you know when you are achieving it?

879. How effective is maintaining the log at facilitating organizational learning?

880. Linked to original objective?

881. Adversarial environment. is your opponent open to a non-traditional workflow, or will it likely challenge anything you do?

882. Decision-making process; how will the team make decisions?

883. With whom was the decision shared or considered?

884. How does provision of information, both in terms of content and presentation, influence acceptance of alternative strategies?

885. How does the use a Decision Support System influence the strategies/tactics or costs?

886. How do you define success?

887. Behaviors; what are guidelines that the team has identified that will assist them with getting the most out of team meetings?

888. Do strategies and tactics aimed at less than full control reduce the costs of management or simply shift the cost burden?

889. Does anything need to be adjusted?

890. What are the cost implications?

3.5 Quality Audit: Chief Revenue Officer

891. Is there a written corporate quality policy?

892. How does your organization know that its relationships with relevant professional bodies are appropriately effective and constructive?

893. It is inappropriate to seek information about the Audit Panels preliminary views including questions like why do you ask that?

894. What are the main things that hinder your ability to do a good job?

895. How does your organization know that its staff placements are appropriately effective and constructive in relation to program-related learning outcomes?

896. How does your organization know that its planning processes are appropriately effective and constructive?

897. Is there a risk that information provided by management may not always be reliable?

898. What are your supplier audits?

899. How does your organization know that its teaching activities (and staff learning) are effectively and constructively enhanced by its activities?

900. Can your organization demonstrate exactly how and why results were achieved?

901. How does your organization know that its range of activities are being reviewed as rigorously and constructively as they could be?

902. How does your organization know that its risk management system is appropriately effective and constructive?

903. Have personnel cleanliness and health requirements been established?

904. How does your organization know that its system for ensuring that its training activities are appropriately resourced and support is appropriately effective and constructive?

905. How does your organization know that its systems for providing high quality consultancy services to external parties are appropriately effective and constructive?

906. What does an analysis of your organizations staff profile suggest in terms of its planning, and how is this being addressed?

907. How does your organization know that its system for examining work done is appropriately effective and constructive?

908. How does your organization know that the range and quality of its accommodation, catering and transportation services are appropriately effective and

constructive?

909. Does everyone know what they are supposed to be doing, how and why?

3.6 Team Directory: Chief Revenue Officer

910. Decisions: is the most suitable form of contract being used?

911. Do purchase specifications and configurations match requirements?

912. How do unidentified risks impact the outcome of the Chief Revenue Officer project?

913. Where should the information be distributed?

914. Who are the Team Members?

915. Process decisions: which organizational elements and which individuals will be assigned management functions?

916. What needs to be communicated?

917. Contract requirements complied with?

918. Where will the product be used and/or delivered or built when appropriate?

919. How will you accomplish and manage the objectives?

920. Who are your stakeholders (customers, sponsors, end users, team members)?

921. Who will report Chief Revenue Officer project status to all stakeholders?

922. What are you going to deliver or accomplish?

923. Process decisions: do invoice amounts match accepted work in place?

924. Timing: when do the effects of communication take place?

925. Why is the work necessary?

926. Does a Chief Revenue Officer project team directory list all resources assigned to the Chief Revenue Officer project?

927. Who should receive information (all stakeholders)?

3.7 Team Operating Agreement: Chief Revenue Officer

928. Do you post any action items, due dates, and responsibilities on the team website?

929. Did you determine the technology methods that best match the messages to be communicated?

930. Do you call or email participants to ensure understanding, follow-through and commitment to the meeting outcomes?

931. Conflict resolution: how will disputes and other conflicts be mediated or resolved?

932. Has the appropriate access to relevant data and analysis capability been granted?

933. Do you record meetings for the already stated unable to attend?

934. Did you draft the meeting agenda?

935. Do you begin with a question to engage everyone?

936. Methodologies: how will key team processes be implemented, such as training, research, work deliverable production, review and approval processes, knowledge management, and meeting procedures?

937. Communication protocols: how will the team communicate?

938. To whom do you deliver your services?

939. Must your team members rely on the expertise of other members to complete tasks?

940. Are there more than two functional areas represented by your team?

941. Confidentiality: how will confidential information be handled?

942. How does teaming fit in with overall organizational goals and meet organizational needs?

943. Do you determine the meeting length and time of day?

944. Did you delegate tasks such as taking meeting minutes, presenting a topic and soliciting input?

945. What is the anticipated procedure (recruitment, solicitation of volunteers, or assignment) for selecting team members?

946. Do you prevent individuals from dominating the meeting?

947. How will your group handle planned absences?

3.8 Team Performance Assessment: Chief Revenue Officer

948. To what degree will the team adopt a concrete, clearly understood, and agreed-upon approach that will result in achievement of the teams goals?

949. To what degree are the members clear on what they are individually responsible for and what they are jointly responsible for?

950. How hard do you try to make a good selection?

951. How do you encourage members to learn from each other?

952. To what degree does the teams purpose constitute a broader, deeper aspiration than just accomplishing short-term goals?

953. Effects of crew composition on crew performance: Does the whole equal the sum of its parts?

954. If you have criticized someones work for method variance in your role as reviewer, what was the circumstance?

955. Do you promptly inform members about major developments that may affect them?

956. Is there a particular method of data analysis that you would recommend as a means of demonstrating

that method variance is not of great concern for a given dataset?

957. How hard did you try to make a good selection?

958. Individual task proficiency and team process behavior: what is important for team functioning?

959. To what degree do team members agree with the goals, relative importance, and the ways in which achievement will be measured?

960. Lack of method variance in self-reported affect and perceptions at work: Reality or artifact?

961. How do you manage human resources?

962. Can familiarity breed backup?

963. To what degree does the teams approach to its work allow for modification and improvement over time?

964. What do you think is the most constructive thing that could be done now to resolve considerations and disputes about method variance?

965. To what degree are fresh input and perspectives systematically caught and added (for example, through information and analysis, new members, and senior sponsors)?

966. What structural changes have you made or are you preparing to make?

967. What makes opportunities more or less obvious?

3.9 Team Member Performance Assessment: Chief Revenue Officer

968. In what areas would you like to concentrate your knowledge and resources?

969. Did training work?

970. Can your organization rate by exception and assume that most employees are performing at an acceptable level?

971. What are acceptable governance changes?

972. How are training activities developed from a technical perspective?

973. How are evaluation results utilized?

974. How do you make use of research?

975. What is the target group for instruction (e.g., individual and collective or small team instruction)?

976. How are performance measures and associated incentives developed?

977. To what degree can all members engage in open and interactive considerations?

978. What were the challenges that resulted for training and assessment?

979. What specific plans do you have for developing effective cross-platform assessments in a blended learning environment?

980. What is a general description of the processes under performance measurement and assessment?

981. To what degree do team members articulate the teams work approach?

982. To what degree will new and supplemental skills be introduced as the need is recognized?

983. Do the goals support your organizations goals?

984. To what degree are the skill areas critical to team performance present?

985. What is a significant fact or event?

986. Are assessment validation activities performed?

987. To what degree do team members feel that the purpose of the team is important, if not exciting?

3.10 Issue Log: Chief Revenue Officer

988. Is the issue log kept in a safe place?

989. Why multiple evaluators?

990. Do you prepare stakeholder engagement plans?

991. What date was the issue resolved?

992. Do you feel a register helps?

993. Why do you manage human resources?

994. Are you constantly rushing from meeting to meeting?

995. Which stakeholders can influence others?

996. What are the typical contents?

997. How were past initiatives successful?

998. Who were proponents/opponents?

999. Is there an important stakeholder who is actively opposed and will not receive messages?

1000. What is the stakeholders political influence?

1001. Are stakeholder roles recognized by your organization?

4.0 Monitoring and Controlling Process Group: Chief Revenue Officer

1002. Is the program in place as intended?

1003. What do they need to know about the Chief Revenue Officer project?

1004. What will you do to minimize the impact should a risk event occur?

1005. Did you implement the program as designed?

1006. Is there undesirable impact on staff or resources?

1007. How was the program set-up initiated?

1008. Is there sufficient time allotted between the general system design and the detailed system design phases?

1009. How are you doing?

1010. Did the Chief Revenue Officer project team have the right skills?

1011. Have operating capacities been created and/or reinforced in partners?

1012. Is the schedule for the set products being met?

1013. Where is the Risk in the Chief Revenue Officer

project?

1014. In what way has the program come up with innovative measures for problem-solving?

1015. Overall, how does the program function to serve the clients?

1016. Based on your Chief Revenue Officer project communication management plan, what worked well?

1017. How is agile portfolio management done?

4.1 Project Performance Report: Chief Revenue Officer

1018. How can Chief Revenue Officer project sustainability be maintained?

1019. What degree are the relative importance and priority of the goals clear to all team members?

1020. To what degree are sub-teams possible or necessary?

1021. To what degree are the goals ambitious?

1022. To what degree can team members meet frequently enough to accomplish the teams ends?

1023. How will procurement be coordinated with other Chief Revenue Officer project aspects, such as scheduling and performance reporting?

1024. To what degree does the teams work approach provide opportunity for members to engage in fact-based problem solving?

1025. To what degree do the goals specify concrete team work products?

1026. To what degree can the team ensure that all members are individually and jointly accountable for the teams purpose, goals, approach, and work-products?

1027. To what degree are the structures of the formal organization consistent with the behaviors in the informal organization?

1028. To what degree will each member have the opportunity to advance his or her professional skills in all three of the above categories while contributing to the accomplishment of the teams purpose and goals?

1029. To what degree will the approach capitalize on and enhance the skills of all team members in a manner that takes into consideration other demands on members of the team?

1030. To what degree do individual skills and abilities match task demands?

1031. What is the PRS?

1032. To what degree does the team possess adequate membership to achieve its ends?

1033. To what degree will the team ensure that all members equitably share the work essential to the success of the team?

4.2 Variance Analysis: Chief Revenue Officer

1034. Are all elements of indirect expense identified to overhead cost budgets of Chief Revenue Officer projections?

1035. Are significant decision points, constraints, and interfaces identified as key milestones?

1036. Does the scheduling system identify in a timely manner the status of work?

1037. Other relevant issues of Variance Analysis -selling price or gross margin?

1038. How are material, labor, and overhead standards set?

1039. Who is generally responsible for monitoring and taking action on variances?

1040. Are management actions taken to reduce indirect costs when there are significant adverse variances?

1041. Are detailed work packages planned as far in advance as practicable?

1042. Does the contractors system include procedures for measuring the performance of critical subcontractors?

1043. What is the actual cost of work performed?

1044. Are overhead costs budgets established on a basis consistent with the anticipated direct business base?

1045. Are estimates of costs at completion generated in a rational, consistent manner?

1046. Are indirect costs accumulated for comparison with the corresponding budgets?

1047. Are overhead cost budgets established for each department which has authority to incur overhead costs?

1048. What are the actual costs to date?

1049. Is all contract work included in the CWBS?

1050. Contemplated overhead expenditure for each period based on the best information currently is available?

1051. How do you evaluate the impact of schedule changes, work around, et?

1052. How does your organization allocate the cost of shared expenses and services?

1053. Did a new competitor enter the market?

4.3 Earned Value Status: Chief Revenue Officer

1054. If earned value management (EVM) is so good in determining the true status of a Chief Revenue Officer project and Chief Revenue Officer project its completion, why is it that hardly any one uses it in information systems related Chief Revenue Officer projects?

1055. How does this compare with other Chief Revenue Officer projects?

1056. Verification is a process of ensuring that the developed system satisfies the stakeholders agreements and specifications; Are you building the product right? What do you verify?

1057. Where are your problem areas?

1058. When is it going to finish?

1059. Are you hitting your Chief Revenue Officer projects targets?

1060. Earned value can be used in almost any Chief Revenue Officer project situation and in almost any Chief Revenue Officer project environment. it may be used on large Chief Revenue Officer projects, medium sized Chief Revenue Officer projects, tiny Chief Revenue Officer projects (in cut-down form), complex and simple Chief Revenue Officer projects and in any market sector. some people, of course, know all about earned value, they have used it for years - but perhaps not as effectively as they could have?

1061. What is the unit of forecast value?

1062. Validation is a process of ensuring that the developed system will actually achieve the stakeholders desired outcomes; Are you building the right product? What do you validate?

1063. Where is evidence-based earned value in your organization reported?

1064. How much is it going to cost by the finish?

4.4 Risk Audit: Chief Revenue Officer

1065. How can the strategy fail/achieved?

1066. Is risk an management agenda item?

1067. Management -what contingency plans do you have if the risk becomes a reality?

1068. Does your auditor understand your business?

1069. Is there a clear procedure for reporting accidents/injuries?

1070. Are end-users enthusiastically committed to the Chief Revenue Officer project and the system/product to be built?

1071. Are formal technical reviews part of this process?

1072. Do you promote education and training opportunities?

1073. Does the team have the right mix of skills?

1074. Is Chief Revenue Officer project scope stable?

1075. Do requirements put excessive performance constraints on the product?

1076. What are the commonly used work arounds in high risk areas?

1077. Is the auditor truly independent?

1078. For this risk .. what do you need to stop doing, start doing and keep doing?

1079. What is the Board doing to assure measurement and improve outcomes and quality and reduce avoidable adverse events?

1080. Have top software and customer managers formally committed to support the Chief Revenue Officer project?

1081. Are some people working on multiple Chief Revenue Officer projects?

1082. Does the customer understand the process?

1083. Are the software tools integrated with each other?

4.5 Contractor Status Report: Chief Revenue Officer

1084. Are there contractual transfer concerns?

1085. What process manages the contracts?

1086. What is the average response time for answering a support call?

1087. What was the overall budget or estimated cost?

1088. How does the proposed individual meet each requirement?

1089. Who can list a Chief Revenue Officer project as organization experience, your organization or a previous employee of your organization?

1090. Describe how often regular updates are made to the proposed solution. Are corresponding regular updates included in the standard maintenance plan?

1091. How is risk transferred?

1092. What was the actual budget or estimated cost for your organizations services?

1093. What was the budget or estimated cost for your organizations services?

1094. What was the final actual cost?

1095. How long have you been using the services?

1096. If applicable; describe your standard schedule for new software version releases. Are new software version releases included in the standard maintenance plan?

1097. What are the minimum and optimal bandwidth requirements for the proposed solution?

4.6 Formal Acceptance: Chief Revenue Officer

1098. What was done right?

1099. Does it do what client said it would?

1100. Was the sponsor/customer satisfied?

1101. Who would use it?

1102. Do you perform formal acceptance or burn-in tests?

1103. Was the Chief Revenue Officer project work done on time, within budget, and according to specification?

1104. Have all comments been addressed?

1105. What function(s) does it fill or meet?

1106. Do you buy-in installation services?

1107. Is formal acceptance of the Chief Revenue Officer project product documented and distributed?

1108. Was business value realized?

1109. What are the requirements against which to test, Who will execute?

1110. Did the Chief Revenue Officer project achieve its

MOV?

1111. Did the Chief Revenue Officer project manager and team act in a professional and ethical manner?

1112. How does your team plan to obtain formal acceptance on your Chief Revenue Officer project?

1113. Do you buy pre-configured systems or build your own configuration?

1114. What features, practices, and processes proved to be strengths or weaknesses?

1115. What can you do better next time?

1116. Was the Chief Revenue Officer project goal achieved?

1117. How well did the team follow the methodology?

5.0 Closing Process Group: Chief Revenue Officer

1118. Did the Chief Revenue Officer project team have enough people to execute the Chief Revenue Officer project plan?

1119. Was the user/client satisfied with the end product?

1120. Just how important is your work to the overall success of the Chief Revenue Officer project?

1121. Is there a clear cause and effect between the activity and the lesson learned?

1122. How critical is the Chief Revenue Officer project success to the success of your organization?

1123. Did the delivered product meet the specified requirements and goals of the Chief Revenue Officer project?

1124. Were cost budgets met?

1125. Were risks identified and mitigated?

1126. What could have been improved?

1127. Will the Chief Revenue Officer project deliverable(s) replace a current asset or group of assets?

1128. Is the Chief Revenue Officer project funded?

1129. What is the risk of failure to your organization?

1130. What can you do better next time, and what specific actions can you take to improve?

1131. When will the Chief Revenue Officer project be done?

1132. Were the outcomes different from the already stated planned?

1133. What areas were overlooked on this Chief Revenue Officer project?

1134. What do you need to do?

1135. Can the lesson learned be replicated?

5.1 Procurement Audit: Chief Revenue Officer

1136. Does the individual having check-signing responsibility review the use of the signature plates?

1137. Is the procurement Chief Revenue Officer project efficiently managed?

1138. Which are main risks and controls of each phase?

1139. Is there no evidence of unauthorized release of information or seemingly unnecessary contacts with bidders personnel during the evaluation and negotiation processes?

1140. Is the procurement function/unit organized the most appropriate way taking into consideration the actual tasks which the department has to carry out?

1141. Does the department have a procurement strategy and is it implemented?

1142. Is the appropriate procurement approach being chosen (considering for example the possibility of contracting out work or procuring low value items through a specific low cost procuring system)?

1143. Is sufficient evidence required for all disbursements (except nominal amounts)?

1144. Are periodic audits made of disbursement

activities?

1145. Where required, did candidates give evidence of complying with quality assurance standards?

1146. Do all requests for materials, supplies, and services require supervisors authorization?

1147. Are existing suppliers that have a special right to be consulted being contacted?

1148. Are individuals with check-signing responsibility prohibited from signing blank checks?

1149. Has your organization examined in detail the definition of performance?

1150. Is confidentiality guaranteed during the whole process?

1151. Are there policies regarding special approval for capital expenditures?

1152. Has an upper limit of cost been fixed?

1153. Budget controls: does your organization maintain an up-to-date (approved) budget for all funded activities, and perform a comparison of that budget with actual expenditures for each budget category?

1154. Are there inferior competencies among procurement staff?

1155. Was the formal review of requests to participate or evaluation of bids correctly undertaken?

5.2 Contract Close-Out: Chief Revenue Officer

1156. How does it work?

1157. Have all contract records been included in the Chief Revenue Officer project archives?

1158. Have all acceptance criteria been met prior to final payment to contractors?

1159. Have all contracts been closed?

1160. Was the contract type appropriate?

1161. How is the contracting office notified of the automatic contract close-out?

1162. Was the contract complete without requiring numerous changes and revisions?

1163. Was the contract sufficiently clear so as not to result in numerous disputes and misunderstandings?

1164. Change in attitude or behavior?

1165. What is capture management?

1166. Have all contracts been completed?

1167. What happens to the recipient of services?

1168. Are the signers the authorized officials?

1169. Parties: who is involved?

1170. Change in knowledge?

1171. Change in circumstances?

1172. How/when used ?

1173. Has each contract been audited to verify acceptance and delivery?

1174. Parties: Authorized?

5.3 Project or Phase Close-Out: Chief Revenue Officer

1175. What are they?

1176. What are the informational communication needs for each stakeholder?

1177. Did the delivered product meet the specified requirements and goals of the Chief Revenue Officer project?

1178. What were the actual outcomes?

1179. What are the mandatory communication needs for each stakeholder?

1180. Planned remaining costs?

1181. What stakeholder group needs, expectations, and interests are being met by the Chief Revenue Officer project?

1182. When and how were information needs best met?

1183. Who controlled the resources for the Chief Revenue Officer project?

1184. What is this stakeholder expecting?

1185. What were the goals and objectives of the communications strategy for the Chief Revenue

Officer project?

1186. What are the marketing communication needs for each stakeholder?

1187. Is the lesson based on actual Chief Revenue Officer project experience rather than on independent research?

1188. Who is responsible for award close-out?

1189. If you were the Chief Revenue Officer project sponsor, how would you determine which Chief Revenue Officer project team(s) and/or individuals deserve recognition?

1190. Who exerted influence that has positively affected or negatively impacted the Chief Revenue Officer project?

1191. What hierarchical authority does the stakeholder have in your organization?

5.4 Lessons Learned: Chief Revenue Officer

1192. How was the Chief Revenue Officer project controlled?

1193. What would you change?

1194. What is the impact of tax policy?

1195. What is your overall assessment of the outcome of this Chief Revenue Officer project?

1196. What is the growth stage of your organization?

1197. What are the funding priorities for intelligence?

1198. What is the frequency of personal communications?

1199. How mature are the observations?

1200. Overall, how effective were the efforts to prepare you and your organization for the impact of the product/service of the Chief Revenue Officer project?

1201. What did you do right?

1202. What is the frequency of communication?

1203. How did the estimated Chief Revenue Officer project Budget compare with the total actual expenditures?

1204. What is your organizations performance history?

1205. What were the major enablers to a quick response?

1206. What is the quality and content of communication?

1207. What are the internal fiscal constraints?

1208. What is the distribution of authority?

Index

activity 5-6, 27-28, 135, 159, 165, 167-169, 171, 173, 175, 179, 182, 185, 187, 261
actual 28, 148, 151, 192, 200, 252, 257, 263-264, 267-269
actually   30, 34, 185, 212, 254
acumen   71
addendum   116
addition   202
additional   27, 50, 52, 59, 99, 113-114, 190
additions   81
additive   98
address   1, 18, 20, 22, 54, 72, 183
addressed   70, 175, 229, 236, 259
addressing   31, 120
adequate   54, 147, 149, 157, 186, 214, 217, 250
adequately   27, 165
adjusted   234
adjusting   149
adopted   90, 99, 130
adopters   205
adoption   115
advance   83, 250-251
advantage   1, 53, 70, 115, 196
advantages   91, 124, 171
advent 109
adverse   251, 256
advise 2
Advisory   230
affect 58, 98-99, 131, 134, 154, 157, 213, 229, 231-232, 242-243
affected   129, 142, 217, 223, 268
affecting   13, 56, 93, 99
afraid 200
against 33, 163, 191, 219, 259
agencies   214
agenda   79, 93-94, 138, 240, 255
aggregate   40, 49
agreed   37, 40, 150, 217, 221
Agreement   7, 240
agreements   253
airline 97, 118
airlines 95, 118
airports 95
alerting   150
alerts   84, 107

include	45, 146, 166, 217, 220, 251
included	4, 9, 94, 105, 110, 181, 189, 225, 252, 257-258, 265
includes	11, 38
including	27, 31-32, 74, 166, 235
inclusion	90, 133
income	95
increase	107, 129, 213
increases	98, 106
increasing	124, 233
Incurrence	200
in-depth	10, 12
indicate	42, 87, 199
indicated	84
indicators	74, 145, 162, 193, 211
indirect	188, 200, 251-252
indirectly	3
individual	75, 124, 137, 167, 199, 243-244, 250, 257, 263
industrial	213
industries	49
industry	1-2, 39, 41, 75, 95, 97, 107, 112, 115-116, 118, 165, 171, 218, 221
industrys	118
inferior 264	
influence	21, 137, 141, 202, 233-234, 246, 268
influences	142, 205
inform 242	
informal	250
informed	200
ingrained	82
inherent	63
inhibit 69	
in-house	2
initially 91, 151	
initiated	190, 231, 247
Initiating	4, 137
initiative	12, 197, 224
injuries 255	
Innovate	62
innovation	57, 78, 98
innovative	181, 189, 248
in-person	129
inputs 26, 35, 79, 140	
insecure	124

market 44, 81, 86, 88, 91, 93-95, 97, 110, 113, 121, 143, 171, 209, 252-253
marketable   209
marketer   9, 21
marketers   59, 70, 98
marketing   21, 41-43, 51, 64, 66-67, 69-70, 72-73, 88, 92-94, 96, 99-104, 107-109, 111-112, 114-118, 123, 125, 130-132, 134, 194, 268
markets   19, 28, 82, 113, 119, 130
material   171, 219, 251
materials   3, 115, 117, 264
matrices   154
Matrix 4-7, 142, 154-155, 195, 199, 213
matter 25
matters   20, 233
mature 269
maturity   60, 133
maximise   128
maximum   137
meaning   170
measurable   29, 31
measure   4, 11, 21, 25, 28, 36, 41, 43, 45, 49, 62, 143, 145, 189-193, 195, 226
measured   41, 66, 79, 195, 216, 243
measures   40, 42, 44-45, 74, 87, 193, 197, 244, 248
measuring   94, 251
mechanical   3
mechanics   230
mechanism   159
mechanisms   145
mechanized   218, 221
mediated   240
medical   86
medium   130, 253
meeting   25, 28, 30, 78, 92, 114, 117, 131, 138, 191, 228, 233, 240-241, 246
meetings   26, 30, 35, 100, 138, 234, 240
member   7, 30, 92, 101, 107, 205, 227, 244, 250
members   1, 26-28, 30-31, 34, 89-90, 123, 130, 149, 165, 185, 203, 206, 214, 217, 238, 241-245, 249-250
membership   250
memories   114
mentor 90

should 9, 19-20, 25, 34, 37, 51, 54, 57, 64, 70, 75-76, 78, 92, 95,
97, 101-103, 106, 112, 119, 129, 131, 141-142, 157, 163, 167-168,
171, 177, 179, 182, 191-192, 201, 210-211, 213, 219-220, 225, 238-
239, 247
-should 192
shrinking   117
signal 64
signature   263
signatures   175
signers 265
signing 264
similar 33-34, 49, 169, 195, 206, 218
simple 253
simply 10, 81, 234
single 49, 69, 163, 187
single-use   9
situation   2, 21, 36, 183, 187, 209, 253
skills   19, 43, 46, 63, 70, 73, 81, 100, 127, 132, 137, 180, 203,
207, 245, 247, 250, 255
sluggish   117
smaller 63
smooth 135
soccer 1
social 26, 78, 98, 112, 116, 123-124, 143
society 121
software   52, 110, 138, 148, 153, 165, 188, 194, 217, 225-
226, 256, 258
solicit 30
soliciting   241
solution   1, 43, 62-69, 71-74, 76-77, 215, 257-258
solutions   40, 65-66, 68-69, 72, 75, 83, 85
solving 22, 249
Someone   9
someones   242
something   97, 157
source 7, 49, 110, 215, 219
sources   49, 53, 60, 73, 89, 118, 125, 153, 211
special 87, 126, 139, 264
specialty   28
specific   10, 18, 29, 31, 45, 97, 119, 170, 173, 175, 187, 201,
213, 219, 228, 231, 245, 262-263
specified   162-163, 199, 216, 261, 267
specify 163, 249

Made in the USA
Middletown, DE
28 April 2022

64825713R00189